display for all seasons
a thematic approach to teaching with children
from five to nine

04

judith makoff and linda duncan

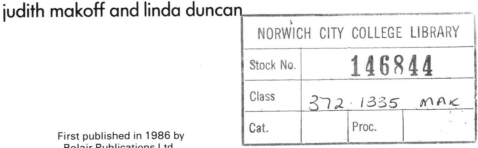
First published in 1986 by
Belair Publications Ltd.,
P.O. Box 12, Twickenham, England TW1 2QL
© Judith Makoff and Linda Duncan
Cover design by Laurence Dunmore
ISBN 0 947882 04 9

Printed and Bound in Hong Kong by World Print Ltd

acknowledgements

The authors would like to thank the following for their co-operation:

The Headmistress, staff and children of Heathfield Infants' School, Twickenham, Middlesex, and to the Education Department, Borough of Richmond-upon-Thames.

The Head Teacher, staff and children at Shortwood County First School, Staines, Middlesex (Surrey North-East Area).

contents

introduction

This book is a collection of seasonal display ideas, embracing the whole infant curriculum. The ideas and illustrations in the book are all taken from our own work as infant teachers with infant children. The line drawings are intended to be only *representative* of children's work.

We feel that infant display should include *all* aspects of children's work where relevant—writing, maths, science and artwork.

All children have a valuable contribution to make to a display, and can be involved in the planning and decision-making at all stages, e.g. in choosing colour and size of backing paper, colour scheme of the display, arrangement of the material, collecting items for the display table, finding suitable books and so on.

As far as possible, the work in the display should be the children's own, rather than a teacher-drawn outline to be 'filled in'.

The teacher's role is a vitally important one of stimulating and encouraging ideas and discussion, providing an appropriate range of working materials and giving guidance and advice. It is essential that the work is carefully planned in advance so that all the necessary resources and materials are at hand.

It is important that we as teachers show children that we value their work. This involves careful mounting or backing of individual pieces of work, thoughtful use of colour, shape and texture, and imaginative arrangement of work to achieve the best effect. It also involves paying attention to details such as :

- using a staple gun rather than drawing pins;
- careful lettering, either in bold felt tip pen, or in cut-out letters, as shown in some of the photographs;
- appropriate labelling of displays;
- sometimes finishing off a display board with an attractive border;
- creating an interesting display table, ideally beneath the display board, perhaps terracing the display table with boxes arranged under the covering fabric;
- creating a 3D effect on the display board.

The finished display should be attractive and eyecatching. It should invite children to stop, look, touch, talk, question and think. It should give the children a sense of pride in their achievement, and the awareness that it really is *their* work.

Judith Makoff and Linda Duncan

daffodils

Discussion and Observation/Science Ideas

Observe the colour, shape, scent, size and parts of the daffodil. Visit local parks or gardens to observe the habitat.

Art and Craft

Individual pictures in different media: paint, chalk, crayon, tissue and fabrics in different shades of yellow. 3D work—egg box trumpet.

Maths

Measure and compare heights; groups of 6 petals.

Other Language Ideas

- Find ten ways to describe a daffodil, e.g. 'A daffodil is . . .'
- Talk about varieties.
- Find other words beginning with 'd'.

Poems and Rhymes

'Daffodils' by W. Wordsworth.
'Daffydowndilly', Traditional rhyme.

Songs and Music

'It happens each Spring', *Harlequin.*

Display Board

Incorporate daffodil pictures into a general spring display as shown above, or as described below.

Green background—yellow paper border. Individual pictures with narrow borders of yellow, black or white. A poem about daffodils. 'Daffodils'—yellow lettering on green.

Display Table

Covered in green/yellow fabric or paper. Vase of daffodils. Book of children's writing about daffodils; books about Spring flowers.

frogs

Discussion and Observation/Science Ideas

Visit local pond or stream and collect frogspáwn to hatch in tank. Observe and record stages of growth and development in the life cycle of frog: colour, shape, size, habitat, food, noises.

Art and Craft

Create a large class picture of pond.

Background: pale blue paper, colour-washed in pale green. Border of white, with black dots to represent frogspawn.

Waterweed: painted on backing with fine brushes, rollerprint sheets of paper in blues/greens and cut or tear waterweed strips. Crêpe or tissue strips. Green lametta, cellophane or foil paper.

Waterlilies: lightly crumpled yellow tissue centres; white paper petals curved and glued around edge. Green paper leaves.

Frogspawn: Bubble packing with black dot in centre.

Tadpoles: Painted, or cut out of black gummed paper, cellograph or dustbin liners.

Frogs: Painted, and printed for skin texture; 3D frogs from junk, plasticine and clay.

Other Language Ideas

- 'Frog' words on tadpole shapes: hop, croak, spawn, bulge, slimy, wriggle.
- Other words beginning with 'fr'.
- Write a story . . . 'I am a frog'.
- Rhyming story or poem.

Music-Making

Experiment with making croaky frog sounds—use guiro, notched sticks, sandblocks, football rattles.

Movement

Frog movements—jumping, hopping.

Books and Stories

The Frog Prince, Traditional.
Tiddalick, The Frog Who Caused a Flood, Robert Roennfeldt, Puffin.
The Tiny Tiny Tadpole, H. E. Todd, Carousel.
Pond Life, Macdonald Starters.

Poems and Rhymes

The Tadpole, E. E. Gould,. *The Book of a Thousand Poems*.
Porwigles, Julie Holder, *First Poetry Book*.
The Frogs Lament, Aileen Fisher, *First Poetry Book*.

Songs and Music

'Five Little Speckled Frogs', *Appuskidu*.
'Kitty Alone', *Second Sixty Songs for Little Children*.

Display Board

as above

Display Table

Terraced, covered in blue/green fabric, or cover fabric with draped clingfilm or polythene. Tank with frogspawn and waterweed, frog models, toy frogs; garden rocks for frogs to sit on, draped with paper weeds; frog books; children's concertina books on frog's life cycle.

blossom

Discussion and Observation/Science Ideas

What is blossom? Which trees have blossom? Discuss colours, shape of flowers, scents, look at different trees in blossom. Re-visit when the blossom has gone. Look at developing fruit/seed case.

Art and Craft

Individual blossom trees in brown and shades of pink and white.

Tree: torn or cut brown tissue, torn pieces of brown textured paper, brown fabric; or thick paint combed finely into bark patterns.

Blossom: tiny torn pieces of tissue, lightly crumpled; flaked rice or coconut coloured with tiny amounts of pink colour, scattered onto glued branches; printing in pink and white paint using pencil-ends; chalk drawings.

Other Language Ideas

'Tree' words—branch, twig, flower, bud, petal, pollen etc.; tree names; words beginning with 'bl'.

Books and Stories

Books about trees.

Poems and Rhymes

'The May Tree', Norah Hussey *Happy Landings*.
'Apple Blossoms', Helen Adams Parker, *The Book of a Thousand Poems*.
'Pink Almond', Katharine Tynan, *The Book of a Thousand Poems*.

Songs and Music

'The Gooseberry Blossoms', Country dance tune (from *The Cuckoo's Nest*, Book 1, David Hindley).

Picture to look at

'Verger—Arles, 1888'. Van Gogh.
'Fruit Trees in Blossom, Spring 1888', Van Gogh.

Display Board

Individual pictures on pink paper (or white, colour-washed pink). Pictures backed on contrast—black, deeper pink, white, OR—giant blossom tree. 'Blossom'—white lettering, decorated by children with blossom, on pink.

Display Table

Pink fabric, blossom branches, books about trees. Products with 'blossom' fragrances—apple blossom talc, soap etc.

eggs

Discussion and Observation/Science Ideas

If possible, borrow incubator and eggs. What hatches out of eggs? Different kinds of eggs—insect eggs, fish eggs etc. Compare sizes, shapes, colours and pattern on shells. Crack egg and talk about the inside. Discuss development of chick or baby bird in egg and how it hatches.

Art and Craft

Decorating hens' eggs—dyes, food colourings, wax resist, felt tips, marbling—also stick on paper shapes, glitter, sequins and then varnish. Egg shell mosaics: paint eggshells first and coat with PVA when dry.

Decorate paper or card egg shapes—thick crayons, marbling, foils and sequins; wet paper with paint dripped on; felt pens, pastels.

Large papier mâché Humpty Dumpty (around balloon)—decorated with paint and fabric.

Maths

Graphs of favourite ways of eating eggs; dozens, half dozens; oval shapes.

Other Language Ideas

Describe eggs on egg-shaped paper. Magic egg stories—'What would you like to come out of your magic egg?'

Outdoor Activities

Egg and spoon race, egg rolling.

Books and Stories

'Pancakes and Painted Eggs', Jean Chapman, Hodder & Stoughton.
'Meg's Eggs', Helen Nicoll, Jan Piénkowski, Picture Puffins.

Poems and Rhymes

'Eggs are Laid by Turkeys', Mary Ann Hoberman, *Rhyme Time*.
'Humpty Dumpty', Traditional.
'Egg Thoughts', Russell Hoban, *All in a Day*, Ladybird.

Songs and Music

'Gathering the Eggs', Lucille F. Wood and Louise B. Scott, *Singing Fun*.
'Rolling down the hill', Ruth Norman, *Action Songs for Special Occasions*.
'The Naughty Hen', *Sixty Songs for Little Children*.

Display Board

Pale pink background, darker pink crêpe border. Individual egg pictures, backed in black or violet; 3D effect on some eggs, achieved by sticking matchbox on back. Each letter of 'eggs' marbled. Egg writing and words on egg shapes.

Display Table

Cover in pink paper or fabric. Display of decorated eggs; toy eggs, nesting eggs; real Easter eggs, large and bite-sized.

the cuckoo

Discussion and Observation/Science Ideas

Collect pictures of cuckoo. If possible visit museum to see the cuckoo and its eggs. Listen to recording of cuckoo's song. Talk about its use of other birds as foster parents: where it lives; size and plumage; the cuckoo as a 'sign of spring'. Bring in and demonstrate cuckoo clock.

Art and Craft

Individual pictures of cuckoo, using different methods of making feathers: single overlapping strips of paper or fabric, stuck down at one end; V-shaped piece of stiff card used to print overlapping feathers; wood shavings; wax 'scraper' pictures or wax resist.

Other Language Ideas

Find some more words with the 'ck' sound.
Factual writing about the cuckoo.

Music-Making

Children's own 'cuckoo' music on chime bars, xylophone, glockenspiel. Could add other bird songs with different instruments.

Books and Stories

Books about birds

Poems and Rhymes

'To the Cuckoo', William Wordsworth.
'The Cuckoo', Dorothy and John Taylor, *Memory Rhymes*.
'The Cuckoo She's a Pretty Bird', Old Folk Song.

Songs and Music

'Cuckoo! Cuckoo!' *Harlequin*.
'Cuckoo', *Third Sixty Songs for Little Children*.
'Sing Cuckoo', *Third Sixty Songs for Little Children*.
'The Cuckoo's Nest', Morris Dance Tune (from *The Cuckoo's Nest* Book 1, David Hindley).

Display Board

Large picture of baby cuckoos in nest with other baby birds being fed by surrogate mother bird. Blue sky background. Tree branches: either painted corrugated cardboard; bark-rubbing collages; sponge printing or combed paint. Leaves: cut out of fabrics and paper in different greens. Nest: stick on twigs, grass, straw, bits of wool. Cuckoos: overlapping layers of fringed paper for feathers. Painted or crayonned head and beak. Cuckoo poem next to board. 'The Cuckoo'—yellow lettering on blue.

Display Table

Green cover, model cuckoos in plasticine, clay, painted papier mâché, using pipe cleaners or matchsticks for legs and beaks. Toilet roll bodies glued on, with fringed layers of paper, paper head and beak. Bird books.

bluebells

Discussion and Observation/Science Ideas

Visit areas where bluebells grow abundantly; bring in large bunch to look at. Use viewers and magnifying glass for close examination. Talk about shape, colour, scent and habitat.

Art and Craft

Colour mixing: shades of blue as close as possible to the actual bluebell. Use, with green, for 'impressionist-type' pictures of a mass of bluebells—small strokes of thick green for leaves, tiny daubs of blue for flowers (best soon after visit to woodlands where there are plenty in flower). Sort out fabric and paper scraps to find similar blue for collage. Individual flower pictures with crayons, pencils, chalks (on black or white); delicate bell-shaped blue tissue pieces arranged on green tissue stem. Bell-printing patterns (shape cut into potato).

Bell stencils in different shades of blue.

Maths

Counting bells per stem; sorting into groups.

Other Language Ideas

Jumbled flowers: jumble names of different flowers, e.g. seor, yill, cutterbup.

Think of flowers beginning with different sounds, or filling in missing letters, e.g. bl__b_l_.

Books and Stories

Flower books.

Poems and Rhymes

'Bluebells', Olive Enoch, *Come Follow Me.*
'Bluebells', P. A. Popes, *The Book of a Thousand Poems.*

Songs and Music

'In and Out Those Dusty Bluebells', D. Taylor, *Dancing Rhymes.*
'Bluebells of Scotland', Traditional.

Display Board

Background: shades of blue. Children's pictures and artwork mounted in white, black or deeper blue. 'Bluebells'—blue lettering on white.

Display Table

Covered in blue or white material. Book of children's writing, books about Spring flowers, viewers and magnifying glass, vase of bluebells. Display of bells.

maytime

Discussion and Observation

Discuss origins of May Festivals, why they were celebrated, traditions such as maypoles and dances, going 'a-Maying', May Queens and May blossoms.

Art and Craft

Paintings of maypole dancing.

Large frieze of maypole, either in picture or 3D.

If latter: use dowelling or broom handle, one end sunk in bowl/bucket of Plaster of Paris. Stick lengths of bright ribbon to top. Place maypole on display table, also few upturned bowls (mounds for sitting on). Cover whole with green fabric (to represent village green). Children bring dolls and teddies to 'dance' and 'watch'—or make rolled-newspaper people wound with pink crêpe, heads of scrunched, taped and painted paper; features painted on. Tape head to body, which is then 'dressed'.

Other Activities

Children's own May Queen procession outside, with crowning, May songs, Maypole dancing; juice or milk to drink.

Poems and Rhymes

'The Maytree', Norah Hussey, *Happy Landings*.
'Maytime', Christina Rossetti, *Young Puffin Book of Verse*.
'May Song', Thomas Nash, *The Merry-go-Round*, Puffin, Penguin Books.

Songs and Music

'The Maypole', *Third Sixty Songs for Little Children*.
'May Morning', Harlequin.
'Floral Dance' (Helston Furry Dance), Traditional.
'Shepherds' Hey' (Old Morris Dance), (both from *Easiest Country Dance Tunes*, Eleanor Franklin Pike).
'Come Lasses and Lads', Traditional.

Display Board

As described above—additional display, or as part of 3D scene—dress doll as May Queen, on throne, attendants crowned with paper flowers. Surround with vases of hawthorn blossom. 'Maytime'—pale pink lettering on darker pink.

rain

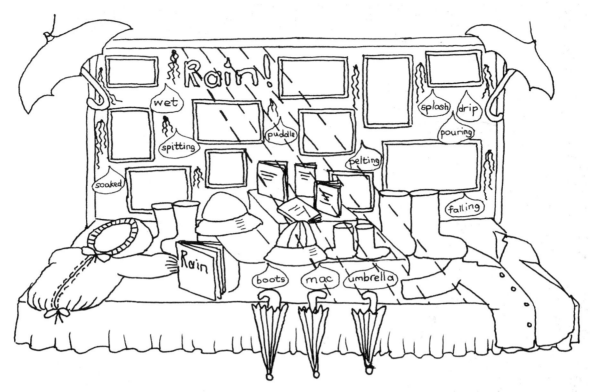

Discussion and Observation/Science Ideas

What is rain? Where does it come from? Why do we need rain? What does it feel like? Go out (suitably dressed!) in rain. How does rain change appearance, feel and smell of things around us? Talk about thunder and lightning.

Art and Craft

Individual pictures of rain scenes—suggested rain techniques: grey paint in fine lines; grey wool; printing with edges of card in parallel lines; silver glitter, foil or cellophane for puddles.

Wet-look pictures: drawings of people, using thick crayon or permanent felt tips—wet the paper, then apply drops of thin watercolour over paper.

Noah's Ark pictures.

Collage of rainwear: cut out of catalogues, magazines and plastic carrier bags.

'Raining cats and dogs'—fun pictures.

Cloud and raindrop pictures—clouds from grey and white bunched tissue or thin pieces of polystyrene; raindrops from paint, or cut from tissue, variety of shiny papers, foils and plastic bags.

Umbrella pictures: design own umbrellas in thick crayons, felt tips.

Maths

Collect rainwater in clean container and measure how much falls over period of time. Chart on graph. Pairs of boots, sorting into sizes and colours.

Other Language Ideas

- Writing: Does rain spoil fun?
- What can we do in the rain?
- Rain words—e.g. splash, trickle, drizzling, pelting, shower, thunderstorm.
- Words that rhyme with 'rain'.

Books and Stories

Postman Pat's Rainy Day, John Cunliffe and Celia Berridge, Hippo Books. Scholastic.
Rain, Peter Spier, Collins.
Rain, Macdonald Starters.

Poems and Rhymes

'John had great big waterproof boots on', A. A. Milne, *Christopher Robin Verse Book*, Methuen.
'It's Raining, it's Pouring', Traditional.
'In the Rain', René Cloke, *Young Puffin Book of Verse*.

Songs and Music

'Pitter Patter Pit Pat', Carey Bonner, *Child Songs*.
'I Hear Thunder', Traditional.
'Singing in the Rain', Arthur Freed and Nacio Herb Brown.
'Splish Splash', *Sing a Song One*.

Pictures to look at

'The Church of Notre Dame at Moret after Rain', Sisley, 1894.
'Les Parapluies', Renoir, *c.*1884.

Display Board

Grey background with silver paper border. Letters of word 'rain' cut out of silver paper, backed in black. 'Rain' words written on white and backed in black. Individual pictures backed in narrow border of black, bright red or yellow.

Rain effect: lengths of taut string painted dark grey in sections. Staple one end to top of board and other to front of display table. Dangle silver lametta or shredded cellophane.

Display Table

Cover with shiny grey lining fabric or similar. Terraced effect with boxes underneath. Display of children's rainwear; books about rain; book of children's 'rain' writing. Hang toy, or children's umbrellas from ceiling.

babies

Discussion and Observation/Science Ideas

What is a baby? Compare human babies briefly with animal babies—gaining independence, feeding, growing. Invite mothers to bring in own babies to show, answer questions and demonstrate feeding, winding, changing, bathing. Bring in and talk about equipment, bedding, clothes and toys. Talk about children's own baby sisters and brothers and what they like or dislike; roles of health visitors, doctor, clinic, midwife. Pre-birth: Discuss how baby grows, develops, is born. Antenatal visits: Invite midwife or a pregnant mother to talk to children about care.

Art and Craft

Cut out pictures of baby items from catalogues and magazines to make collages—under separate headings of 'Feeding', 'Sleeping', 'Getting About', 'Dressing', 'Bathing'. Collage of baby faces with different expressions when sleeping, crying etc.

Pictures of babies—use paint, crayon, chalk or felt tip. Pictures of scenes of baby's day—bath, meal, outings, play. Collage and junk models, from labels, empty packs and boxes of baby products.

Lifesize model of baby: head—papier mâché over balloon. Paint, then seal with PVA and glue on features; rolled-newspaper limbs covered with glued pink tissue or paper, and painted pink; stuffed stocking body; dress in baby clothes.

Maths

Chart comparing each child's birthweight or lengths at birth.

Capacity—how many eggcupsful/teaspoonsful of water fill a baby's bottle?/How many bottles of water fill a jug, bucket, bowl?

Chart of favourite baby foods.

Other Language Ideas

Writing on 'My Baby Sister/Brother/Cousin' or 'My Friend's Baby'. Why do babies cry?

Missing words: e.g. 'A baby sleeps in a __ (cot, hat)'.

Play and Drama Activities

Equip home corner with baby equipment and baby dolls, including baby bath, nappies, talc and cream, clothes, towel, old feeding equipment.

Cookery and Tasting

Bring in samples of ready-cooked baby food or prepare own ingredients to taste and discuss; also talk about other foods babies can have, and the importance of hygiene.

Books and Stories

101 Things to do with a Baby, Jan Ormerod, Kestrel.
Baby's Catalogue, Janet and Allan Ahlberg, Picture Puffins.
Peepo! Janet and Allan Ahlberg, Picture Puffins.
Emma's Baby Brother, Gunilla Wolde, Hodder & Stoughton.
The New Baby, Camilla Jessel, Methuen.

Poems and Rhymes

'Baby', *Nothing Solemn*, Hippo.
Be Nice to a New Baby, Helen Oxenbury and Celia Berridge,
Book of Manners, Picture Puffin.
'Bye Baby Bunting', Traditional.

Songs and Music

'All for Baby', M. I. Fletcher and M. C. Denison, *High Road of Song*.
'What Shall I do with the Baby Oh?' Anna Mendoza and Joan Rimmer, *30 Folk Settings*.
'John Brown's Baby', *Okki Tokki Unga*.

Pictures to look at

Selection of 'Madonna and Child' portraits through the ages, including those by Dürer, Titian, Renoir, Raphael.

Display Board

Background—chequerboard pattern of alternate sheets of pink and blue paper. Border of halved doilies. 'babies'—white on black paper. Pictures mounted on black or deeper shades of pink or blue. Baby clothing items and pink and blue bows stapled to board.

Display Table

Cover in pink and/or blue. Baby equipment brought in by children. Life-size model of baby or baby doll in baby chair. Feeding equipment; toys in basket; powders and creams. Books on baby care; stories; factual books for children about babies and family relationships. Book of photographs of some children or teachers as babies.

rabbits

Discussion and Observation/Science Ideas

What do they look like? Discuss their habits, food, colour, feel, habitat, movements. Look at real rabbits in pet shops, or a child's own. Talk about rabbit care. Are rabbits pests?

Art and Craft

Line drawings of visiting rabbit using chalk, crayon, pastel, felt tips. Collages of rabbits, using cotton wool, mohair wools, soft-textured fabrics and pile fabrics, e.g. velours, towelling, brushed fabrics, fur fabrics—some on previously painted backgrounds of sky and grass, sealed with diluted PVA, others cut out for display board.

Junk models of rabbits, painted and sealed with diluted PVA.

Maths

Chart of class rabbit's preferred foods each day.

Weigh and measure rabbit weekly—note growth.

Other Language Ideas

Other words beginning with 'r'.

Display Board

Pale blue sky, overprinted with sponges, or rag-rolled in slightly deeper blue. Grass—printing different shades of green on green paper, using corrugated cardboard. Rabbits—collage, painted, drawn—stapled on.

Display Table

Terraced and covered in green fabric and paper. Display of rabbit models and children's toy rabbits; rabbit story books and pet care books. Saucers of rabbit food (labelled). Book of children's rabbit writing or rabbit stories.

Find little words in 'rabbit'—e.g. rat, rib, bat.

Factual writing about rabbits.

Movement/P.E.

Rabbit-like movements—bunny-hopping, nose-twitching, paw movements while washing and grooming.

Books and Stories

Mr Rabbit and the Lovely Present, Zolotow/Sendak, Puffin.
Morning, Rabbit, Morning, Mary Caldwell, Hodder & Stoughton.

Poems and Rhymes

'See the Little Bunny Sleeping', *This Little Puffin*.
'Bunny Rabbit', anon, *The Book of a Thousand Poems*.
'The Rabbit', Edith King, *The Book of a Thousand Poems*.
'A Little Brown Rabbit', *This Little Puffin*.

Songs and Music

'Run Rabbit Run', Traditional.
'Lippity Lop', *High Road of Song*.
'Rabbit Ain't Got', *Appiskidu*

Picture to look at

'Young Hare', Albrecht Dürer.

easter bonnets

Discussion and Observation

Why do we have Easter bonnets? Collect photographs of any previous local Easter Bonnet Parades from newspapers or magazines; talk about hats, hat shapes, ideas for trimming and decorating; ways of fastening on decorations. Hold Easter Bonnet parade, with songs.

Art and Craft

Provide variety of bright and gaudy bits—card, papers, nets or other 'floaty' fabrics, scarves, paint, old ties, crayons, lace, ribbons, sequins, beads, plastic fruit or flowers, boxes, glue, string, sticky tape etc. Decorate Easter Bonnets, either using any old hat or cap as basis, or making hat from paper or card.

Maths

Sorting hats by colour, shape, size, decoration. Find heaviest or lightest hat; tallest or widest. Matching hats to wearers—jumbled pictures of hats (drawn or cut out of magazines) and wearers on large card. Put up on wall for children to discuss.

Display Board

On wall: fullsize paintings of each child in Easter bonnet. On board: bright backing—orange or yellow, with stripey border. Individual Easter bonnet/hat pictures, backed in narrow border of black or contrasting colour; Easter bonnets stapled to board.

Other Language Ideas

Writing—Describe your Easter bonnet.
Vocabulary—*either* other 'hat' words (cap, helmet, beret, deerstalker, mob cap) *or* vocabulary associated with decorating bonnets: paint, flower, beads, glue etc.

Books and Stories

Old hat, new hat, Stan and Jan Berenstain, Collins.

Poems and Rhymes

'The Quangle Wangle's Hat', Edward Lear, Picture Puffin.

Songs and Music

'My Easter Bonnet', *Harlequin.*
'Where did you get that hat?' *Jolly Herring*
'The Saint Wears a Halo', by 'Peter', *The Book of a Thousand Poems.*

going on holiday

Discussion and Observation/Science Ideas

Talk about different sorts of holiday—at home, seaside, country, abroad, hotel, caravan, farm, canal etc. and ways of getting there—car, train, coach, plane, boat, hovercraft. What do you take on holiday? Who packs? Are you excited? What sort of food do you have on the journey? How do you pass the time? (games, books etc.) Introduce vocabulary—travel agents, journey, ticket, motorway, take off, land, sail, depart, arrive etc.

Art and Craft

Individual pictures—paintings, crayonning, felt tips, magazine collages, fabric collages—transport, family packing, arriving at destination, holiday activities.

Maths

Graphs: most popular kinds of holiday/accommodation/transport.

'Pack'—cut out suitcases with specific number of items of clothing/toys (cut out from catalogues) e.g. 2 pairs of shoes, 4 shirts etc.

Time: Time taken to get there.

Display Board

Background—sheets of red and yellow, arranged in chequerboard design, or one bright plain colour. Border of bright crayonned paper flags. Individual pictures backed in narrow border of black, white or toning colour. Some arranged as train, as shown, with children's drawings of passengers here and there.

Display Table

Bright fabric to match board, terraced with boxes at one end. Display of children's toys—bus, cars, Fisher-Price Playpeople and luggage, aeroplanes, trains, boats; books about holidays or transport—airports, harbours or stations.

Times of day: Talk about timetables, 24-hour clock.

Weight: bring in travel bags, small suitcases. Weigh them empty and with a few items inside.

Other Language Ideas

Children can write about their last holidays, plus minor disasters, e.g. breakdowns, travel sickness, missing train/plane/boat; Mum and Dad being cross etc.

Books and Stories

Talkabout holidays, Margaret West, Ladybird.
The little car has a day out, Leila Berg, Pan.
The little engine that could, Watty Piper, Collins.
Books about different countries.

Music and Songs

'Pack up your troubles', *Ta-ra-ra boom-de-ay.*
'A Holiday in Spain', *Harlequin.*
'Wheels on the Bus', *Sing a Song One.*
'Morningtown Ride', *Appuskidu.*

Poems and Rhymes

'Four little girls', A. E. Dudley, *Happy Landings'*
'The holiday train', Irene Thompson, *The Book of a Thousand Poems.*

at the seaside

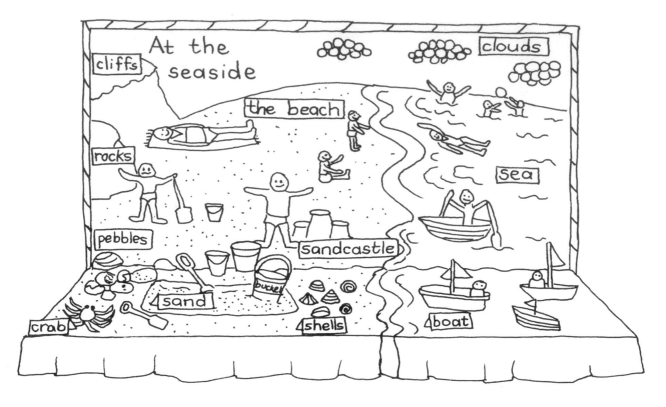

Discussion and Observation/Science Ideas

Who has been to the seaside? What do you like to do at the seaside? Look at sand and talk about what it feels and looks like. Discuss pebbles, shingle, shells, crabs, shrimps, rockpools, the sea, its tides (ebb and flow), rocks and cliffs, donkey rides, buckets and spades, sand castles. What do you take to the seaside? What do you wear? Show large map of British Isles and talk about resort names—names of children who have been to a resort could be attached to the map.

Art and Craft

Individual pictures—shell collages, sand patterns (paint PVA onto paper, sprinkle on sand and tap off excess.) Seaside pictures with swirly sea effects—marbling, roller-painting in wave patterns, finger patterns. Sand glued on or mixtures of lentils/split peas/pasta to represent pebbles or shingle. Paintings/drawings/crayonnings of children at the seaside. Wax resist—crayonning of people/children on the beach over-washing with yellow paint.

Display Board

Blue sky, bubble-printed white clouds (or circular yoghurt pots). Grey sponge-printed cliffs. Sand—sheets of sandpaper or painted yellow paper with lightly sprinkled sand glued on. Sea—sheets of marbled paper in greens, blue and white—crayonned, painted or fabric collage people on beach and in sea. Bright stripey border around board.

Display Table

Carry on 'beach' with yellow fabric—paper sprinkled with sand, Fill large cat litter tray with sand. Disguise edges of tray with yellow paper or fabric, and sprinkle with more sand. Display rocks, shells, beach toys, crabs. Continue 'sea' in similar way to display board, or use sea-green fabric. Display children's toy or made boats.

Maths

Graphs—How many children have been to the seaside? Sorting, counting, classifying and threading shells. Weighing shells. Weight and volume of sand and water.

Other Language Ideas

Things to see/feel/hear.

Books and Stories

Harry at the Seaside, Gene Zion/Margaret Graham, Bodley Head.
Seaside Maths, Macdonald Starters.

Poems and Rhymes

'At the Seaside', R. L. Stevenson, *Rhyme Time.*
'There are big waves', E. Farjeon, *Once Upon a Rhyme.*

Songs and Music

'I do like to be beside the seaside', *Ta-ra-ra boom-de-ay.*
'Take me to the seaside', *Harlequin.*

Picture to look at

'At the seaside', Degas, 1876.

daisies

Discussion and Observation/Science Ideas

Pick a few daisies with stalks. Observe carefully under a magnifying glass. Note shape of leaves, tinges of pink, and shape of petals. Talk about other flowers in daisy family—sunflowers, golden rod, dahlia, michaelmas daisy. Make daisy chains.

Art and Craft

Draw carefully with white chalk on black. Paint with thin brushes on black or green.

Tissue paper petals and yellow fabric/fur/towelling centre.

Pasta daisies—long grain rice petals—centres of yellow split peas/lentils—glued on black paper.

Stalks and leaves—fabric, paper or noodles.

Daisy prints—ovals and circles in white, yellow and green on contrasting fabric or paper.

Maths

Make a number line using cut out daisies 1–100.

Other Language Ideas

Describe a daisy—'A daisy is . . .'; think of words with the 'ai' sound; write a story about a magic daisy.

Books and Stories

Books about wild flowers.

Poems and Rhymes

'The field daisy', Jane Taylor, *The Book of a Thousand Poems*.
'The daisy', James Montgomery, *The Book of a Thousand Poems*.
'Daisies and grasses', Anon, *The Book of a Thousand Poems*.

Songs and Music

'Daisy, Daisy', *Appuskidu*.
'A little daisy showed its head', Carey Bonner, *Child Songs*.

Display Board

Background in golden yellow or emerald green. Border of printed or paper daisies. 'Daisies'—white on green or white on yellow to contrast with background. Pictures backed in black, white, yellow or green, again as contrast to background. Daisy poem. Collection of items, with daisy patterns or motifs, stapled to board (handkerchiefs, scarf, shawl etc.).

Display Table

Cover to match or complement board. Box under table cover to focus attention on vase of daisies. Daisy greeting cards, tea towels, decorated boxes, china, a daisy chain, book of children's writing, flower books.

baby animals

Discussion and Observation/Science Ideas

Visit a farm. Talk about animals and babies: a baby cow is a calf, etc. Discuss how the mother cares for baby; appearance when newborn, feeding, washing, how appearance changes; behaviour, growth and development.

Art and Craft

Individual pictures of baby animals.
Lambs: cotton wool, rolled or fringed and curled paper; white textured fabrics. Thick white paint, combed into swirls.
Chicks: Yellow fur fabric, crumpled tissue, tiny pieces of yellow sponge, sponge printing with yellow paint.
Calves: Thick crayon; paint with coat of dilute Marvin or varnish when paint is dry; oil pastels or conté crayon—rust brown, black and white.

Maths

Numbers in each litter; two-legged and four-legged animals.

Number language—heaviest, lightest, big and small etc.

Shape work—as in 'Pigs' display shown above (children cut out own circles, triangles and oblongs).

Other Language Ideas

Anagrams: e.g. bmla=lamb
Animal stories on animal-shaped paper.

Music-Making

Experiment with making animal sounds with voices and home-made instruments—make rhythm patterns.

Movement

Animal mimes—lambs frolicking, piglets rooting and rolling etc.

Books and Stories

Said the First Little Chick, Gareth Williams, Fontana Picture Lions.
Feeding Babies, Chiyoko Nakatani, Picture Puffins.

Poems and Rhymes

'Three Little Pigs and a Little Pig More', *This Little Puffin*.
'Lambs at Play', C. Rossetti, *The Book of a Thousand Poems*.

Songs and Music

General animal and farm songs.

Display Board

As shown above, *or* pale blue sky, printed with ends of toilet rolls in thick blue and white paint. Grass—green paper with card edges, in different shades of green. Deeper green border painted with white daisies. Individual pictures of animals stapled on; e.g. pigs in mud in corner of field (brown paint mud with coat of PVA). 'Baby animals'—white lettering on yellow.

Display Table

Covered in green fabric, terraced with boxes. Toy animals, animal junk models, books.

the sun

Discussion and Observation/Science Ideas

The sun is a star. Why does it not look like a star? Is the sun always there? What happens at night time? Why do we need the sun? Talk about shadows. What makes a shadow? Where does the sun have to be? Talk about sundials.

Art and Craft

Large sun: made by colour mixing yellow and red. Start with red at centre, add yellow in increasing quantities to outside of circle. Add gold rays.

Individual suns: yellow sponge prints, wax crayons or pastels. Add gold rays. Pasta suns sprayed gold. Paint with different shades of yellow. Wax resist—orange and yellow. Print in yellows.

Collage: glitter and sequins.

Maths

Collect spherical objects.

Other Language Ideas

'Sun' words: sunflower, sunrise, sunset, sunglasses, sunhat, Sunday.
'Sun' vocabulary: rays, sunny, sizzle, heat, shines, dazzles etc.

Display Board

Background—red paper as illustrated and described above (border using marbling technique). 'The Sun'—yellow lettering on black.

Display Table

Table covered in orange and yellow fabric. Books about the sun. Collection of round or spherical objects.

Books and Stories

The Sun and the Wind, Traditional.
Sunshine Jan Ormerod, Kestrel.
Arrow to the Sun, Gerald McDermot, Picture Puffins.

Poems and Rhymes

'The Summer Sun', Wes Magee, *A Very First Poetry Book*.
'The Sun's Travels', R. L. Stevenson, *A Child's Garden of Verses*.
'My shadow', R. L. Stevenson, *A Child's Garden of Verses*.

Music and Songs

'The Sun has got his hat on', *20 All Time Junior Hits*, Butler/Gray.
'Sun Arise', *Tinderbox*.
'One Two Three', *Tinderbox*.

Pictures to look at

'Impression, Sunrise', Monet.
'The Church of Notre Dame in Sunshine', 1893, Sisley.

under the sea

Discussion and Observation/Science Ideas

What do the children think it's like under the sea? What things could they expect to find? How do divers breathe underwater? How do fish breathe? Discuss fish, seaweed, pebbles, mermaid's purse, rocks etc.

Art and Craft

Individual pictures: marbling in blues/greens/turquoise. Make fish collages, to stick on top; or try crayonning fish thickly, then apply marbling on top. Seaweed—green, blue or silver, stuck on in clumps; strands of wool, fringed green crêpe or tissue. Pebbles—sponge-print paper with various yellow ochres and browns. Also dowel print.

Large pictures/frieze: Sea background—marbled or sponge prints in blues/greens covered in cling film or cellophane. Rocks—grey sugar paper formed into 'rocks'—painted greys. Sea bed—print 'pebbles' as above. Border—'seaweed' stapled around the edge. Fish—look in books for different sorts of fish to copy for anatomy and colours, or—fantasy fish—decorate as desired with a variety of materials—paints, crayons, scales cut out of foils, tissues, papers and fabrics, sequins etc.

Display Board

As illustrated above (see Art and Craft section). 'The Sea'—green lettering on blue foil. Write 'sea' words around board on fish shapes.

Display Table

Cover table with something shiny if possible—lining material in green, blue or turquoise (boxes underneath for terraced effect). Collect pebbles, shells etc. Fish books.

Maths

Octopus—1 octopus has 8 tentacles
          2 octopuses have 16 tentacles

Other Language Ideas

Write 'fishy' stories on fish-shaped paper.
Think of other 'sh' words.
Write about different fish.

Books and Stories

The Sea, Macdonald Starters.
Under the Sea, Macdonald's First Library.
The Little Mermaid, Hans Andersen.

Poems and Rhymes

'The flattered flying fish', E. V. Rieu, *The Puffin Quartet of Poets*.
'Here is the Sea', *This Little Puffin*.

Songs and Music

'Appuski dusky', *Appuskidu*.
'I do like to be beside the seaside', *Ta-ra-ra boom-de-ay*.
'Three Jelly Fish', *This Little Puffin*.
'Until I saw the sea', *Tinderbox*.

Pictures to look at

'Rough Sea, Etretat', Monet, 1883.

poppies

Discussion and Observation/Science Ideas

Bring in bunch of poppies or look at some growing. Where do they grow? Identify parts using magnifying glass.

Art and Craft

Individual poppies—bright red paint, coated with PVA when dry. Black stippled centre or crumpled/rolled tissue. Red/orange tissue paper petals. Fabric centre. Individual pictures of poppy field: grass—printed with edge of card in shades of green. Poppies—finger-printed on to grass, or 'dabbed' on with brush. Draw poppies with crayons or felt tip—observing as much detail as possible.

Maths

Draw poppy on squared paper—find area.

Display Board

Yellow background, border of poppies, or white background with red crêpe border. Individual pictures mounted on black or red. Poem at side. 'Poppies'—white lettering, decorated with poppies by children, on red.

Display Table

Yellow fabric, or red fabric with red/white print as shown. Books on flowers. Vase of real poppies or tissue paper poppies.

Other Language Ideas

Write about growth of poppy from seed to plant in a zig-zag book.

Books and Stories

Flowers, Life Cycle Books, Althea, Longman.

Poems and Rhymes

'Poppies', P. A. Popes, *The book of a Thousand Poems*.

Songs and Music

'Poppies dance in the cornfield', *Harlequin*.

Pictures to look at

'Poppy Field', Monet.

sunflowers

Discussion and Observation/Science Ideas

The sunflower is one of the daisy family. Discuss shape, height, petals, seeds, habitat. Plant some and watch them grow.

Art and Craft

Large sunflower: marbled petals, bubble packaging painted brown/ochre for seeds.

Individual sunflowers:
Petals: printed in shades of yellow; yellow paper or fabric collage, or apply thick paint with glue spreader, 'sunburst' fashion.

Centres: brown/yellow tissue; circles of thick paint; pasta sprayed gold, or bubble packaging painted brown.

Maths

Record growth. Measure height of sunflowers at intervals.
Concepts: as tall as a ....
           taller than ....
           shorter than ....
Count petals.
How long does the flower last?

Display Board

Background—mustard coloured paper. Orange crêpe border. Van Gogh's 'Sunflowers' print backed in dark brown. Sunflower pictures.

Display Table

Matching or toning fabric or paper cover. Children's own sunflower plants.

Other Language Ideas

Sunflower—Make little words—sun, flower, no, flow, flew, on, run, nose.

Books and Stories

'The Sunflower and the Rosebush', *Little Storyteller, No. 6* Marshall Cavendish.

Pictures to look at

'Sunflowers', Van Gogh.
'Sunflowers', Monet, 1881.

buttercups

Discussion and Observation/Science Ideas

Observe colour and number of petals. Discuss habitat, time of year seen, 'Old Wives' tale'—'do you like butter?' Visit a field if possible.

Art and Craft

Large buttercup: yellow paint with coat of PVA.

Individual: tissue centres, thick wax crayon or oil pastel petals.

Field of buttercups: green paper with different shades of green printed with edge of card to give grass effect. Yellow finger prints for buttercup effect.

Maths

Counting in 5's.
Find 2, 3, 4 things smaller than larger than } a buttercup

Display Board

Background—green paper with yellow finger prints. Yellow and white border. Large buttercups displayed on board.

Display Table

Green/yellow material. Bowls of buttercups. Books about summer wild flowers.

Other Language Ideas

Words to describe a buttercup.

Books and Stories

Books about wildflowers.

Poems and Rhymes

'Buttercups', Anon, *The Book of a Thousand Poems*.

Songs and Music

'Daisies are our silver', Traditional.

caterpillars and butterflies

Discussion and Observation/Science Ideas

Find caterpillars and identify parts with viewers or magnifying glasses, let caterpillars crawl on fingers and hands. Talk about what they feel like—colour, size, texture, shape. What is a caterpillar? Life cycle from egg—caterpillar, chrysalis, pupa, butterfly, laying eggs again. What do caterpillars eat? Do people like having them in the garden? Keep a few in large tank with twigs, nettle and other leaves (replaced frequently). Which leaves do they prefer?

Art and Craft

Make caterpillars from egg box sections painted and joined together (threaded). Stick pieces of card on for bristles and feet. Large cabbages from a selection of green papers. Cut large nettle-shaped leaves on which to put eggs (made from plasticine, papier mâché or crumpled tissue balls). Make or paint pupae hanging from leaves. Draw and paint caterpillars as they are seen, paying close attention to detail—felt tips, pencils, crayons, pastels. Make stylised caterpillars out of tissue paper circles overlapped (blue-green) and overprinted with blue/green. Paint on bristles, feet etc.

Butterflies: Make large butterflies to hang from ceiling—fold wet painted paper and cut into butterfly shape. Bright symmetrical patterns and designs either painted, wax crayon, felt tip. Decorate with paper circles, sequins, silky material scraps. Copy real patterns by looking at books, photographs, pictures.

Maths

Make caterpillars by drawing around circles. Number each circle

$$①②③④⑤⑥$$

as above, but colour caterpillar in sequence pattern.
Count pairs of legs, eyes, e.g.
    1 caterpillar has 2 eyes
    2 caterpillars have 4 eyes, etc.
Measure real caterpillars!
Measure made ones, and put in order of size.
Butterflies—link with symmetry (as illustrated above).

Other Language Ideas

Caterpillar words written on caterpillar-shaped paper, e.g.

Other words starting with the same letters
    c—cabbage
    a—apples
    t—tomato
    e—eat
    r—etc.
Make zig-zag books about the life-cycle of a caterpillar.

P.E./Movement

'Caterpillar Creep' (on tape) from 'Watch' BBC Schools programme.

Books and Stories

The Very Hungry Caterpillar, Eric Carle, Picture Puffin.
The Creepy Crawly Caterpillar, H. E. Todd and Val Biro, Carousel.
'Butterflies', Althea, *Life Cycle Books*, Longman.
Butterflies, Macdonald Starters.

Poems and Rhymes

'The Tickle Rhyme', Ian Serraillier, *Roger Was a Razor Fish*.
'The Caterpillar', C. Rossetti, *Come Follow Me*.
'The Butterfly', Margaret Rose, *The Book of a Thousand Poems*.

Songs and Music

'The Butterfly', Country dance tune from Cecil Sharp Collection (*The Cuckoo's Nest*, Bk. 1, David Hindley).
'I went to the cabbages', *Tinderbox*.
'Caterpillars only crawl', *Harlequin*.
'Butterflies', *Second Sixty Songs for Little Children*.
'How does a caterpillar go?' *This Little Puffin*.

Display Board 1. (photograph)

Cover board half bright pink, half white; yellow crêpe border. 'Symmetry' cut out of pink paper on purple. Table, purple/violet mixture.

Display Board 2. (line drawing)

Sky blue background. Children crayon or paint nettles and cabbages, or use paper collage with *lightly* crumpled tissue paper for cabbage leaves, and green papers for nettles; pieces of white fabric or paper for flowers. Vividly decorated butterflies in marbling, wax resist, crayon, bright paints, foil and fluorescent papers, pattern printing—stapled on board and hung from ceiling. Crayonned or painted caterpillars.

Display Table

Green fabric or paper; book of children's writing; model caterpillars; vivarium with caterpillars and leaves for observation (observation chart could accompany this); appropriate books.

going swimming

Discussion and Observation/Science Ideas

Who goes swimming, and how often? Where? Who can swim? Discuss health and safety points—no swimming after a heavy meal, behaving sensibly, being clean, watching for others in trouble and knowing what to do. (RoSPA's publications on the subject). Compare with danger of swimming in the sea—change of tides, temperature, waves, currents etc. Talk about what to wear in the water. Look at pictures of swimming pool and sea with swimmers. Why is a pool safer?

Art and Craft

Individual pictures of children swimming, splashing or playing in the water.

Backgrounds—marbling in blues/turquoise/sea greens; wet paper with water and drop colours on, and allow to dry.

Sponge-prints in above colours: either cover with cling film or a thin coat of dilute PVA for shiny effect. Make figures—paint, crayon or cover with fabric.

Wax resist technique—crayon figures and 'wash' with thin blue-green paint.

Display Board

Light background at top. Children's pictures of spectators and swimmers in crayon or collage—use the kinds of fabric pieces from which swimwear is made. Swimming pool—turquoise paper or paint with layer of shiny PVA when paint is dry; or, marbled sheets of paper with white gloss, and when dry paint over with light wash of turquoise watercolour. Glue figures on top.

Display Table

Shiny turquoise fabric if possible—or blue polythene. Display swim rings, costumes, towels, armbands, books, appropriately labelled.

Maths

Floating and sinking—provide a variety of materials, and make a chart to see which articles float and which sink.

Other Language Ideas

Anagrams of words connected with swimming, e.g. oolp, aes, tukrns, slspah etc.
Write about safety rules.

Books and Stories

Going Swimming, Althea, Dinosaur Publications.
Water Safety, Robert Birch, Ladybird.
Jenny learns to swim, Nigel Snell, Hamish Hamilton.

Poems and Rhymes

'Swimming in the Town', Ian Serraillier, *First Poetry Book*.

Songs and Music

'Three Little Fishes', *Sing a Song One*.
'Oh, Jemima, look at your Uncle Jim', Traditional.

Picture to look at

'Bathing Place at Asnières', the National Gallery, London, Georges Seurat.

keeping cool

Discussion and Observation/Science Ideas

What do we wear in hot weather? Why? Discuss materials, colours, summer patterns. Look at own clothes and in catalogues. Discuss how different members of the family dress in summer. Discuss the body's cooling mechanism—sweating.

Art and Craft

Children paint pictures of themselves—lifesize, by drawing round one another. Dress in summer clothes—suitable fabrics glued on or painted on.

Make: Fans—colour in bright colours.

Ice-creams in plastic sundae glasses—pink/white/yellow cotton wool—stripy straws, red tissue balls for cherries.

Iced lollies—used lolly sticks with card lollies.

Plastic drinks bottles with coloured water.

Sunhats—brimmed.

Parasols—pleated wallpaper, dowel rod.

Maths

Summer shapes (3D and flat).
Make cones—ice cream.
Sorting fabrics by colour and texture.
Symmetry of clothes shapes.

Other Language Ideas

Talk about other ways of keeping cool—fans, parasols, cold iced drinks, ice-creams, water.

Books and Stories

Clothes, Macdonald Starters.
Summer Story, Brambly Hedge, Jill Barklem, Collins.

Poems and Rhymes

'August Afternoon', Marion Edey and Dorothy Grider, *The Young Puffin Book of Verse*, compiled by Barbara Ireson.

Songs and Music

'Mud, Mud', *The Best of Flanders and Swann*.

Pictures to look at

'Women in the Garden', Monet, 1866/67
'A Bathing Place', George Seurat.

Display Board

Plain blue sky and green background. Border of red and white or yellow and white stripes. Children's own figures in bright colours decorated and clothed in paper collage, fabric collage, thick bright crayon, paint. Yellow sun and rays with words in black lettering.

Display Table

Bright fabric in summery pattern, or plain bright yellow. Display of sunhats, sunglasses, empty plastic squash bottles, children's made paper fans, vividly decorated, model ice-cream sundaes, books about Summer or clothes.

bees

Discussion and Observation/Science Ideas

Invite beekeeper in to talk. Discuss different kinds of bees and what they do, how they live, how pollen and nectar is collected, where honey comes from, what bees use honey for, how we get different kinds of honey; beekeepers, the Queen bee. If possible, watch bees in garden or local park, or on film strip. Show how granulated honey can be made liquid again by standing jar in warm water.

Art and Craft

Large picture of bees collecting pollen and nectar from flowers.

Bees: paint, felt tip, crayon, yellow and brown/black fur fabric; wings out of clingfilm or polythene.

Flowers: bright paint, tissue, different papers.

3D bees: covered toilet roll tubes, painted yellow/brown.

Maths

Tessellate hexagons (honeycomb patterns). Look for hexagons elsewhere.
Make equilateral triangles into hexagons.

Display Board

Large picture of bees on flowers—painted, crayonned, marbled and collage. Dangle 3D bees from ceiling or fasten to board here and there. Background—blue (for sky). 'Bees'—yellow on black.

Display Table

Yellow or green fabric: display of bee products—polishes, different honeys (with spoons for tasting), comb honey, beeswax candles; books about bees; children's model bees and own writing about bees in a book. Hexagon patterns and other pictures around board, appropriately labelled.

Other Language Ideas

Vocabulary—nectar, pollen, bee milk, larva, pupa, honey sac, worker bee, Queen bee, hive. Write a sentence using each word.
Other 'ee' words—see, feel etc.

Books and Stories

'Winnie the Pooh and some bees', A. A. Milne, *Winnie the Pooh*, Methuen.
'How the bee became', T. Hughes, *How the Whale became*, Puffin.
Bees make honey, Sarah Allen, Dinosaur Publications.
Bees, Macdonard Starters.

Poems and Rhymes

'Here is the beehive', *This Little Puffin*.
'Isn't it funny', *This Little Puffin*.
'The Queen Bee', Mary K. Robinson, *Come Follow Me*.
'A Swarm of Bees in May', Traditional.
'A bumble bee', Anon, *Rhyme Time*.

Songs and Music

'Flight of the Bumble Bee', Rimsky-Korsakov.
'Song of the Bee', *Sixty Songs for Little Children*.

rainbows

Discussion and Observation/Science Ideas

What is a rainbow? When does it occur? Observe the sequence of colours—red, orange, yellow, green, blue, indigo, violet. Observe colour paddles and filters. Mix colours and make colour spinners.

Art and Craft

Individual paintings, paper collage, fabric collage, printing. Rainbow 'graffito'—wax scraper pictures.

Wax resist—thick crayon rainbow, colour-washed with blue.

Make pictures of each colour using a using a different technique, e.g. red—fabric collage in shades of red. Orange—potato prints, yellow—hand prints etc.

or: painting objects known to be one colour, e.g. post box, bus, yellow sun etc.

Maths

Sorting by colour.
How many red/blue things etc?
Counting in 2's (Noah's Ark)

Other Language Ideas

Write a story with a rainbow theme, e.g. 'The tiny rainbow-coloured mouse' 'The rainbow worm'.
Make little words from the big word, e.g.—in, on, an, ran.

Books and Stories

'Jane's Surprise', *Little Story Teller, 3*, Marshall Cavendish.
Noah's Ark Stories.
Red Riding Hood, Macdonald Starters.
Colour, Macdonald Starters.
Rainbow Colours, Starters Science.

Poems and Rhymes

'The rainbow fairies', Anon, *The Book of a Thousand Poems*.
'I asked the boy who cannot see', Anon, *Once Upon a Rhyme*.
'What is pink?' C. Rossetti, *Once Upon a Rhyme*.

Songs and Music

'Joseph and the Amazing Technicolour Dreamcoat', T. Rice and A. Lloyd-Webber.
'Sing a rainbow', *Appuskidu*.
'Captain Noah and his Floating Zoo'', Michael Flanders, Joseph Horovitz.
'Colours', *Sing as You Grow*, Brenda Piper.

Display Board and Table

Divide both into seven strips; back each strip with fabric or paper in rainbow colours. In each section display (a) on board—pictures and collages in different shades of the same colour; (b) on the table—objects of same colour. Back children's pictures in narrow border of black or white for contrast. Staple border of red or gold around display board. Could also have separate rainbow table displaying rainbow-patterned clothes, carrier bags, stationery, toys, wrapping paper.

COWS

Discussion and Observation/Science Ideas

Visit farm (at milking time if possible) or collect pictures of cows. What do they look like? How big and how heavy are they? What do they do? How do cows make milk? How are they milked—hand/ machine? What happens to the milk? Where does it go? Discuss pasteurisation, milk products, different breeds of cows—Jersey, Guernsey, Alderney. Make butter in jam jars.

Art and Craft

Individual pictures of cows in field—green printed background—yellow and white blobs to represent daisies and buttercups. When dry, paint cow on top or make out of papers, cut into shapes. 3D cows out of boxes and toilet rolls, yoghurt pots.

Maths

Make a graph to show how many children drink milk. Capacity work: litres, pints, half litres.

Other Language Ideas

Find out which other animals give milk. Why is milk good for us?
'ow' words.

Books and Stories

The Cow who fell in the canal, P. Krasilovsky and P. Spier, Picture Puffin
The Sick Cow, H. E. Todd/V. Biro, Puffin.
Milk, Macdonald Starters.

Poems and Rhymes

'Cows', James Reeves, *'The Puffin Quartet' of Poets*.
'The Cow', R. L. Stevenson, *A Child's Garden of Verses'*.
'The King's Breakfast', A. A. Milne, *Christopher Robin Verse Book*, Methuen.
'This little cow eats grass', *This Little Puffin*.

Songs and Music

'Where are you going to, my pretty maid?', *Oxford Nursery Song Book*.
'Our Milkman', *Singing Fun*.

Display Board

Background—blue sky, white sponge-printed clouds. Children's individually drawn, painted, chalked and collage cows. Grass—comb different shades of green paint onto green paper, print with yellow and white dots (finger or pencil ends) for flowers. Clumps of green fringed paper grass.

Display Table

Cover with green fabric, terraced with boxes. Children's 3D model cows, toy cows, milk lorries. Display empty milk product containers, or milking equipment, e.g. stool, churn, pail—or make by covering real bucket with painted paper, card churn and stool. (A parent good at woodwork might help out with stool.) Books about cows, farm animals, milk and dairy products.

teddy bears' picnic

Discussion and Observation/Science Ideas

What is a picnic? Dictionary definition. Discuss children's own experiences on picnics—where they went, what food they took etc. Talk about picnic baskets, cool boxes, flasks, packing away neatly, taking rubbish home. Talk about the places where people go for picnics—beach, woods, park etc. Hold a teddy bears' picnic, with a rosette for each teddy—e.g. oldest teddy, happiest teddy.

Art and Craft

Individual pictures of picnic or own teddy at picnic— paints, crayons, felt tips, fabric collage. Painting or collage of favourite picnic food. Rosettes for teddy.

Maths

Counting teddies, sorting into size, colour, weight, etc. How many sandwiches would be needed for each child in class to have 1 or 2 each? (Crisps, biscuits etc.) Estimate the cost of the above. How many drinks could be made from a bottle of squash/water etc.

Other Language Ideas

Make up a label for rosette for your teddy, e.g.

Make up a menu for a picnic.

Books and Stories

Teddy Bears' Picnic—Althea First Book, Dinosaur Publications.
Spring Story, Brambly Hedge, Jill Barklem.
Wilberforce Goes on a Picnic, Margaret Gordon, Picture Puffin.
Packed Lunches, Kate Hutchinson, Ladybird.
The Wind in the Willows (picnic section) Kenneth Grahame, Methuen.

Poems and Rhymes

'Picnics' (from *Punch*) *The Book of a Thousand Poems*.

Songs and Music

'Teddy Bears' Picnic', J. Kennedy. B. Feldman & Co. Ltd.
Record—'20 All Time Junior Hits', Butler/Gray.

Display Board

Background—blue sky, pale or bright blue. Green grass overprinted with different greens using card edges or using a combing technique. Print flowers with dowel ends, fingertips or paintbrush (fan bristles out on paper by pressing down hard and lifting brush away smartly). Children's paintings or fabric collages of children at picnic.

Display Table

Green fabric, 'landscaped' with scrunched up newspaper underneath, paper or printed flowers on top. Children's own teddy bears round gingham cloth; dolls' tea set, picnic hamper and contents: drinks bottle or flask; books. 'Teddy Bears' Picnic'—yellow on green or white.

wheat harvest

Discussion and Observation/Science Ideas

Visit bakery to see breadmaking. Look at different breads. Send off for samples of stages in wheat milling. Find out how wheat is grown and harvested. Plant wheat berries in spring and watch them grow. Talk about windmills and watermills. Visit mills or look at models in museum.

Art and Craft

Collages using straw. Simple straw weaving—mount finished piece on contrasting paper (dark brown or black).

Paintings and pictures of wheatfields—visit wheatfield or look at picture first. Experiment to find accurate 'wheat' colours. Line drawings of ears of wheat in pencil, white or yellow chalk on black or brown sugar paper, or crayon.

Pictures of foods made with flour; paint, crayon or collages of magazine cut-outs.

Maths

Weigh out flour for recipes. Weigh wheat berries. Volume—e.g. how many cups of wheat/flour fill a bowl? Make bread, rolls, biscuits etc. with different flours; also playdoughs—vary quantities of ingredients and discuss results.

Other Language Ideas

Vocabulary—e.g. combine harvester, tractor, bales, stubble, grain.

Books and Stories

Bread, T. B. Roscoe, Ladybird.
Bread, Macdonald Starters.

Poems and Rhymes

'August', Eunice Fallon, *Come Follow Me*.
'Harvest Song', Anon, *Come Follow Me*.
'Bread', H. E. Wilkinson, *Come Follow Me*.

Songs and Music

'Oats and Beans and Barley Grow', Traditional.
'Harvest', *Harlequin*.

Pictures to look at

'The Corn Harvest', Pieter Breughel, 1565.
'The Harvest', Pissarro, 1882.

Display Board

A corridor display on different boards could cover various stages in harvest process—or just one, as illustrated.

Background—blue sky—could roller or sponge-print shades of blue. Wheatfield—sheets of yellow paper overprinted with different shades of golden yellow and ochre, using edges of card; or use thick paint, 'combed'.

Wisps of real straw, grasses and ears of wheat stuck on with PVA when paint is dry. Tractor—build from boxes, cut-out cardboard wheels and details, then glue and paint. Varnish, or coat with PVA.

Scarecrow—make cross-shape out of sticks or dowelling and bind with string or tape; glue on paper or card face and hat, wool or straw hair. Dress in ragged jacket; add straw wisps. Secure to board by stapling through jacket. Make border of real or paper wheat ears and real corn dollies.

Add *children*'s line drawings of combine harvester, birds etc. to the picture.

Display Table

Cover in natural coloured hessian or golden yellow fabric—preferably with 'rustic' look (open weave or rough texture). Display children's toy tractors and farm machinery, small tied bundle of wheat (or vase with a few ears of wheat) or make wheat with cylinder of painted card and ears of wheat cut from fringed yellow paper. Books about farms, harvest and the story of bread.

the wind

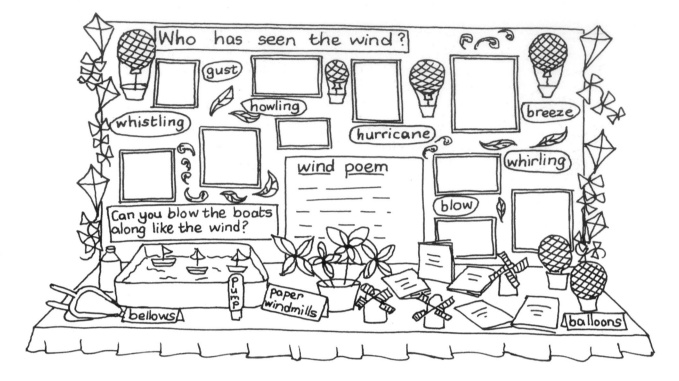

Discussion and Observation/Science Ideas

What is the wind? What does it do/feel like/sound like? Discuss the difference between gales, hurricanes, cyclones, breezes etc. Observe action of the wind on different objects—kites, paper aeroplanes, paper windmills, balloons, washing on a line, trees and grass, clothes—in strong wind and gentle breeze.

Art and Craft

Pictures and paintings of wind blowing trees, hair, clothes etc. Making paper windmills and kites—decorate with thick crayon, wax resist or bright paint. 'Hot air' balloons—net fruitbags over balloons, tied to margarine tubs covered with paper and paint.

Kites—decorate in crayon, printing patterns, sequins, glitter.

Wind effect patterns: blowing paint through straws, or with cold setting of hairdryer; liquid paint squirted with squeezy bottles into patterns.

Maths

Time taken to dry wet dolls' clothes in wind. Which took longest? Why?

Display Board

White or pale blue background marbled with blue/pale grey/white gloss. Pictures backed in black or very dark blue. 'Hot air' balloons. Feathers and leaves stapled to background as if being blown by wind. Children's made kites as border, decorated with vividly crayonned or painted patterns.

Display Table

Blue fabric or paper. Water tray with tiny boats made by the children or small plastic boats. Empty washing up liquid bottle, bellows and balloon pump for experiments with blowing boats along. Made and bought paper windmills and models of mills.

Other Language Ideas

'Wind' words—e.g. gust, breeze, blow, whistling, whirling, howling.

Music-Making

Experiment with objects, instruments and voices to imitate wind sounds—e.g. rustling pasper, rice shakers, blowing across the top of glass bottles; with voices, barely audible, breathy 'ooo/eee' sounds.

Books and Stories

The Wind Blew, Pat Hutchings, Picture Puffin.
Mrs. Mopple's Washing Line, Anita Hewett and R. Broomfield, Picture Puffin.

Poems and Rhymes

'The Wind', James Reeves, *The Puffin Quartet of Poets*.

Songs and Music

'Who has seen the wind?' *Tinderbox*.
'The North Wind', *Harlequin*.

owls

Discussion and Observation/Science Ideas

What sort of creature is an owl? What does it look like? Talk about owl sounds: how food is caught and eaten; different kinds of owl; the origin of the idea of 'wise owl'. Visit museum or bird sanctuary.

Art and Craft

Individual owl pictures—study plumage, markings, colours and patterns. Use fabric for collage—frayed pieces especially good—torn paper strips stuck down at top end; wood-shavings (could be painted when dry); real feathers. Owl puppets from paper bags, old socks, large yoghurt cartons—features stuck, painted or sewn on.

Maths

Owl 'shape pictures'.

Other Language Ideas

'Owl' words. Writing about owls and other *nocturnal* animals. Other words with 'ow' sound: cow, bow, how, tower, flower etc.

Books and Stories

Goodnight Owl, Pat Hutchins, Picture Puffin.
The Owl Who Was Afraid of the Dark, Jill Tomlinson, Puffin.
The Little Owl, Reiner Zimnik, Hanne Axman, Picture Paperback, Methuen.

Poems and Rhymes

'5 Little Owls', Anon, *Roger was a razor fish*, Jill Bennett.
'At Night', Barbara Ireson, *Rhyme Time*.
'The Owl'. Lord Tennyson, *The Book of a Thousand Poems*.

Songs and Music

'The Funny Little Owl', Ruth Norman *Action Songs for Special Occasions*.
'The Owl'. *Sixty Songs for Little Children*.

Display Board

Background—royal blue/dark blue paper. Large tree in textured fabrics, papers, collage, bark rubbing or printing with bark or wood pieces. Individual owls cut out and stapled to branches. Owl poem. Owl words.

hansel and gretel

Discussion and Observation

Read a good version of the story with attractive pictures. Familiarise children with it by discussion, and by any of the suggested activities below.

Art and Craft

Individual pictures of characters in story—painting, collage or crayon.

Maths

Shapes, tessellations—decorations on the Gingerbread House.

Other Language Ideas

Talk about family relationships—including sisters, brothers, step-parents etc.

What is it like to have very little food and money in our country? In the Third World? Long ago, and now?

Music-Making

Children could make up appropriate musical phrases or sound patterns with tuned or untuned percussion for each character as the story is re-told by the children.

Movement/Drama

Mime to story, with or without musical accompaniment.

Books and Stories

'Hansel and Gretel', Yoshitaro Isaka, *Fantasia Pictorial*, Frederick Warne.

Songs and Music

'Hansel and Gretel', Opera by Humperdinck—'Gingerbread Waltz'. 'Witch's Ride', 'Dance Duet', 'Evening Prayer'.

Display Board

Background—back with tinfoil. Staple on painted trees and real twigs, silver lametta, strips of brown and white tissue from branches and top of board.

Gingerbread house—paint large cardboard boxes in squares of bright colours; seal with PVA. Cut window with shutters and a door; paint, frame with cheap biscuits (old stale ones collected by children) or make playdough biscuits, baked hard, painted and varnished. Stick on to house with PVA or Copydex. Also use cheap sweets, bottletops, sweet wrappers, crumpled foils, pictures of biscuits and candy cut out and stuck on; sequins and shapes. Cardboard roof: paper heart-shaped tiles representing gingerbread. Witch's face at window—painted paper or stuffed fabric—green face, purple hair, big teeth.

Display Table

Cover with brown tissue/fabric draped with lametta.

night

Discussion and Observation/Science Ideas

Discuss differences between night and day. What makes it dark? Which do you prefer—night or day? Why? Talk about night fears, dreams, night family routines, going out at night. What can you see and do?

Art and Craft

Outdoor night scenes—houses, street lights and shops drawn in thick, bright crayon, colourwashed in dark blue or black. Paper collage on dark or mid-blue paper; silhouette house shapes with yellow or gold windows; stars; moon. Paintings of night time routines indoors; bedtime, bath, story etc.

Maths

Block graph of bedtimes; compare earliest and latest times—also tea or dinner times or time working parent arrives home; look at 24-hour and 12-hour clocks.

Other Language Ideas

'Night' vocabulary, e.g. dark, shadow, black, mysterious, peaceful, quiet, creeping.

Display Board

Background—purple or royal blue paper. Pictures backed in white, yellow or narrow black and then white (black next to dark background would not provide adequate contrast).

Silver star mobiles: giant pasta moon sprayed silver—or covered with various thick card circles, glued on, then covered with foil and a light smearing of black shoe polish in hollows to give 'relief picture' of mountains and craters. Child-size 'Wee Willie Winkie' painted and cut out on wall next to display board. Night poem or rhyme on his front.

Display Table

Cover with purple or blue fabric or paper. Nightwear, doll in bed, bedside items etc. brought in by children. Books.

Children's free writing about 'night'—after discussion; more specifically, 'Bedtime' or 'Sounds at Night', or 'A dream'.

Books and Stories

Peace at Last, Jill Murphy, Macmillan Children's Books.
Whatever Next, Jill Murphy, Macmillan Children's books.
Bears in the Night, Jan and Stan Berenstain, Collins.

Songs and Music

'Sleep Baby Sleep', Traditional.
'The Moon Song', *Sixty Songs for Little Children*.

Poems and Rhymes

'Wee Willie Winkie', Traditional.
'Night Sounds', Thomas Middleton, *Rhyme Time*.
'Shadow March', R. L. Stevenson, *A Child's Garden of Verses*.

Pictures to look at

'Boulogne Harbour by Moonlight', Manet, 1869.
'Café Terrace at Night', Van Gogh.

witches

Heigh ho for Hallowe'en!

Book of Spells

Discussion and Observation

Discuss children's thoughts and ideas about witches; witches in history; white and black witches; what they are supposed to look like and wear; accompanying paraphernalia—cauldron, broom, spell book, hat etc; Hallowe'en and its traditions.

Art and Craft

Imaginations can run riot with paintings, collages and junk models of witches and cats, bats, owls and seething cauldrons. Plenty of black and vivid fluorescent colours in green, violet, yellow, orange; also sparkles of gold and silver sequins and glitter. Bats and witches cut out and hung as mobiles, or displayed on walls and windows with moon and star shapes in gold and silver foils.

Maths

Counting, weighing and volume—all used in measuring ingredients for spells in cauldron. Children could write down own individual spells, e.,g. 'Put in: 12 teaspoons of sand, 50g. salt, 1 cup of orange squash, 7 leaves' etc. Weigh the resulting mess!

Make shape witches, cut out and stuck on paper, or as 3D models, based on cone shapes.

Other Language Ideas

Write own spells, with ingredients, instructions and magic words, for different occasions, for a book of spells. 'Witchy' words, 'witch' stories, familiar ones re-told in own words, or children's own stories, maybe writing about a witch they have painted or made.

Words ending in 'tch'.

Music-Making

Talk about appropriate music for witches to dance to at Hallowe'en. What instruments can make frightening sounds? (See below for suitable music to listen to for inspiration). Setting witch poem to music using untuned percussion only, or combination of untuned percussion and lower notes of tuned percussion—alto xylophone, deeper notes of recorder, voices—humming and open vowel sounds—ahhh . . . eee . . . oohh . . . all in low register, as drones and chants.

Movement/Drama

Link with music-making in dance to short poem, or story. Use list of 'witchy' words to help, and appropriate gestures and expressions.

Other Hallowe'en Ideas

Make simple food for class Hallowe'en party; give it appropriate names. Dress up as witches, cats or ghosts to perform dance, mime, or songs, to other classes. Have apple-bobbing and trick-or-treat games.

Books and Stories

Meg and Mog stories, Helen Nicoll and Jan Pieńkowski, Picture Puffin.
The Little Witch, Otfried Preussler, Knight Books.
Gobbolino the Witch's Cat, Ursula Moray Williams, Puffin.

Poems and Rhymes

Hist Whist, collected by Dennis Saunders, Piccolo, Pan Books.
'Witch. Witch', Rose Fyleman. *Rhyme Time.*
'The Witches' Ride', Ruth Sansom, *Rhythm Rhymes.*

Songs and Music

'Halloween's Coming', *Harlequin.*
'Spooky', *Harlequin.*
'There was an old witch', *Appuskidu.*
'Gobbolino the Witch's Cat', *Appuskidu.*
'The Sorcerer's Apprentice', Dukas.
'Witches' Sabbat', Berlioz from *Symphonie Fantastique.*

Display Board

Background—royal blue or violet. Gold stars, silver full moon. In cauldron—yellow/green tissue or cellophane; rubber snakes and creepy crawlies brought by children. Fire—gold paper flames—yellow-red fluorescent papers; cellophanes. Sticks on table beneath 'flames'.

Display Table

Labelled nasty ingredients—marbles coated thickly with Vaseline (bats' eyes) cooked spaghetti or macaroni mixed with food colouring (brains or intestines), dish of plastic spiders; slime—liquid paint mixed with liquid soap. Chopped red jelly—blood jelly. Mobiles from ceiling—witch's broom in corner. Table covered with violet or green fabric/paper. Border of black or gold zigzags.

cats

Discussion and Observation/Science Ideas

Compare children's own pet cats or cats they know. Describe them in detail—colour, feel, size etc; feeding, cat care. Bring in cat to observe and feel. Other members of the cat family. Look at pictures of different breeds.

Art and Craft

Pictures of own cats, cats from stories (e.g. 'Gobbolino', 'Mog', 'Puss in Boots', Dick Whittington's cat).

Paintings or line drawings (conté crayons, fine felt tips, crayon, oil pastels), Talk about drawing and painting fur and how best to achieve furry texture.

Fabric collage—sort out fabrics with soft furry feel.

Maths

Chart—how many children have cats?
Cat colours; favourite names; oldest/youngest cats.

Other Language Ideas

Cat names—most and least popular.

'Cat' expressions—'catty', 'cat's whiskers', 'cat who's got the cream'.
Words that rhyme with 'cat'.

Movement/Drama

Imitate a cat's actions—stretching out, washing, stalking, pouncing.

Books and Stories

Puss in Boots, Traditional.
My Cat Likes to Hide in Boxes, Eve Sutton, Picture Puffin.
Cats, Macdonald Starters.
Millions of Cats, Wanda Ga'g, Picture Puffin.

Poems and Rhymes

'Five Little Pussy Cats', *This Little Puffin*.
Old Possum's Book of Practical Cats, T. S. Eliot, Faber & Faber.
'Cat!', Eleanor Farjeon, *Puffin Quartet of Poets*.

Songs and Music

'Pussy Cat, Pussy Cat', Traditional.
'Gobbolino, the Witch's Cat', *Appuskidu*.
'My Cat', *Sing as You Grow*, Brenda Piper.

Display Board

Background—royal blue sky. Dark painted houses with yellow or gold windows stuck on; 3D houses from cereal boxes. Silver stars in sky. Individual cats drawn, painted or fabric collage (any fabric with a pile of soft texture—velvet, corduroy, fleece, fur fabric, wool). Cat poem.

Display Table

Terraced and covered in blue fabric or paper. Collection of cats—toys, pottery, glass and porcelain models, puppets. Books and stories about cats: book of children's writing. Clean, empty cat food tins (no sharp edges), or cat food labels. Book of photographs of children's and teachers' cats.

squirrels

Inside the display:

Whisky frisky
Hippity hop
Up he goes
To the tree-
top!
Whirly, twirly
Round and round
Down he scampers
To the ground.

a baby squirrel is called a kitten.

a squirrel's nest is called a drey.

a squirrel uses his tail as
a blanket   a parachute
a sail   a hook
and to help him balance.

Discussion and Observation/Science Ideas

Discuss the meaning of 'mammal' and 'rodent' and the differences between red and grey squirrels—their habitat, appearance and mannerisms. Listen to squirrel sounds in woods. Observe feeding and scampering.

Art and Craft

Careful drawings from observation; in park, museum, or from pictures. Paintings of squirrels in trees.

Experiment with ways of achieving fur effect—paint combing, brushing with toothbrush or fork. Fabric collages with textured pile fabrics (velours, plush, cord, towelling, fleece). Paper collage.

Printed squirrels—child draws squirrel shape and prints with corrugated card, sponge or cottonwool.

Squirrel puppets in fur fabric, felt, socks, jumper sleeves.

Maths

Make cards: 1 to 1 correspondence—e.g. give every squirrel 1 nut.

More/less—e.g. 'give 1 squirrel two more nuts'.
Weigh nuts, acorns, horse chestnuts.

Other Language Ideas

Words beginning with 'squ'.
Factual writing and observations.

Movement

Squirrel-like movements—sudden, jerky, fast, darting, light.

Books and Stories

Mrs. Squirrel and Hazel, Jane Pilgrim, Hodder & Stoughton.
Squirrels, Brian Wildsmith, OUP.

Poems and Rhymes

'The Squirrel', Liliam Moore, *Rhyme Time*.
'10 Little Squirrels', *This Little Puffin*.
'Mr. Squirrel', V. M. Julian, *Come Follow Me*.
'Whisky Frisky', Anon. *The Book of a Thousand Poems*

Songs and Music

'Squirrel Nutkin', *Second Sixty Songs for Little Children*.
'Hunting the Squirrel', Morris Dance Tune (from *The Cuckoo's Nest*, David Hindley).

Display Board

Background—yellow paper printed in Autumn colours, using toilet rolls or yoghurt pots. Could make drey out of real leaves and tissue paper, stapled to background. Individual squirrels using paint, tissue or fabric collage.
Leaves—cut out tissue shapes or marbled paper leaves. Border of leaves in Autumn colours. 'Squirrels'—yellow lettering on red.

Display Table (not illustrated)

Yellow, orange or rust cover: children's squirrel models, finger and glove puppets; books, dishes of acorns, pine cones and chestnuts.

picking apples

Discussion and Observation/Science Ideas

Describe apples—using all senses. How and where are apples grown? Discuss harvesting, apple products and recipes, different varieties and colours. Make apple dishes—stewing and baking, toffee apples, in crumbles—try different (non-alcoholic) apple juices.

Art and Craft

Draw or paint apples, trying to match colours accurately, using crayon, pastels or coloured pencils (felt tips probably too crude in colour).

Cut in half horizontally and draw outline and pattern in centre.

Apple prints, with rejected windfall apples; using green/red/russet and yellow shades; apple-leaf prints on paper or fabric.

Apple shape collages in appropriate coloured smooth papers or fabrics.

Maths

Try growing pips of different varieties. Label pots. Observe and record growth.

Weigh apples. Cut into halves, quarters, segments.

'Count the apples on a tree' theme as teaching aid—twig in a pot of earth with paper apples to hang from loops; or tree painted on card, covered in coverfilm; children stick on card appples painted red, yellow or green with blobs of 'Blu-Tack'.

Other Language Ideas

Words beginning with 'a'; other words containing a double consonant; re-telling story of Adam and Eve in own words.

Books and Stories

Adam and Eve
'One Eye, 2 Eyes, 3 Eyes', Traditional.
Apples, Macdonald Starters.
'The Big Red Apple', *Time for a Story*, Eileen Colwell, Young Puffin.
'The enormous apple pie', Diana Ross, *Stories for 6 year olds*, Puffin.

Poems and Rhymes

'If I were an apple', Anon., *Rhyme Time*.
'Apple Harvest', Helen Leuty, *The Book of a Thousand Poems*.

Songs and Music

'Old Roger', *Okki Tokki Unga*.
'Sucking Cider Through a Straw', *Ta-ra-ra boom-de-ay*.
'Upon Paul's Steeple', *Faber Book of Nursery Songs*.

Pictures to look at

'The Apple Pickers, Eragny', Pissarro, 1885.
'Apples and Pomegranates' (Still Life), Courbet.

Display Board 1.

Backed in red or green or red and green chequerboard. Individual apple pictures backed in black and white.

Display Table

Growing apple pips (with chart); scales for weighing and balancing apples; books, apple drinks, 'apple' cosmetics—shampoo, face masks etc., tinned apple products, wicker baskets of apples—real or papier mâché.

Display Board 2.

Large picture of apple-picking. Large tree with card branches and twigs or rolled/painted newspaper branches stretching over ceiling: dangling card applies and paper leaves—fringed green crêpe paper wound round branches or individual paper leaves stuck on. 'Picking apples'—red lettering on yellow. Apple mobiles from ceiling.

hedgehogs

Discussion and Observation/Science Ideas

Discuss where and how they live; their colour, size and food; the function of their prickles; the feel of the animal. What else is prickly?

Art and Craft

Make hedgehogs—use apple or potato halves, dough, clay, papier mâché; cocktail sticks or spent matchsticks for prickles. Paint or stick on facial features.

Individual hedgehog pictures—background first in Autumn colours, then when dry paint hedgehogs on top, with leaves round about (real or painted). Handprinted prickles, or print with stiff card.

Paper collage—with layers of fringed black or brown paper, bent upwards at right angles to paper.

Maths

'Prickly' shapes and patterns—zigzags, wide and narrow. Triangle patterns on hedgehog shape in gummed paper. Make cards, e.g. '1 hedgehog has 8 prickles'; '2 hedgehogs have 16 prickles' *or* 'Put 5 prickles on the hedgehog'/'6 prickles on the hedgehog' etc.

Other Language Ideas

Make small words from 'hedgehog'.
Descriptive writing on hedgehog-shaped paper.
Decorate edge.
Zigzag books of 'hedgehog' stories.

Movement

Shuffling, curling up tight at given signal, moving close to ground.

Books and Stories

Smith the Lonely Hedgehog, Althea, Dinosaur Publications.
'Hans, My Hedgehog', Grimm.

Poems and Rhymes

'The Hedgehog', Ian Seraillier, *Rhyme Time*.
'The Hedgehog and his Coat', Elizabeth Fleming, *Come Follow Me*.
'The Hedgehog', Edith King, *The Book of a Thousand Poems*
The Prickly Little Hedgehog (Nature Activity Readers). Look Books Series, Philograph Publications.

Songs and Music

'Good Morning, Mr. Hedgehog', *Nursery Songbook*, Winifred E. Barnard.

Display Board

Background of either hessian, or yellow or orange paper. In centre, giant cut-out hedgehog textured in crumpled brown and black tissue on oval shaped black paper. Paint on black prickles afterwards round edge. Individual pictures round edge, cut out. 'Hedgehogs'—orange/red letters on dark brown.

Display Table

Cover in matching or toning fabric. Edging, in brown or black paper stapled to bottom of fabric. Model hedgehogs; books; tray of other 'prickly things'.

autumn leaves

Discussion and Observation/Science Ideas

Discuss different kinds of deciduous trees. Collect with the children a variety of leaf shapes and colours, and identify them. Teacher can make card templates for future use.

Art and Craft

Leafprints in warm Autumn colours—shades of reds, oranges, yellows, browns, golds.

Paint *around* leaf shapes.

Leaf collages—child or teacher cuts out leaf-shapes in variety of papers—tissue, gummed, wallpapers, wrapping-paper etc. in Autumn colours; also red and gold foils, red and yellow cellophanes.

Paintings of trees with falling leaves—after observation if possible; or use thin twigs, glued on paper then stick on leafprints and paper leaves.

Leaf rubbings in crayon.

Prolong freshness of real leaves on pictures or as mobiles by coating both sides with dilute PVA medium.

Maths

Sort and group leaves by shape, size or colour, e.g. jagged edges, bumpy edges, long thin leaves etc.

Other Language Ideas

Tree names.
Descriptive words for appearance of leaves.
'Leaf' sounds—crunchy, crackly, swishing etc.
Other words with 'ea' sound.

Movement

Leaves blown by wind—light, floating, whirling and swaying movements.

Books and Stories

Leaves, John Leigh-Pemberton, Ladybird Leaders.
Look at Leaves, Macdonald Starters.
Leaves from Trees, Althea's Nature Series, Dinosaur Publications Ltd.

Poems and Rhymes

'Five Little Leaves', *This Little Puffin*.
'Autumn', Florence Hoatson, *Rhyme Time*.
'What the leaves said', Anon, *Rhyme Time*.

Songs and Music

'Falling Leaves', *Singing Fun*.
'The Autumn Leaves', *This Little Puffin*.
'The Leaves are Green', *Dancing Rhymes*.

Picture to look at

'The Market Cart', Thomas Gainsborough, 1786.

Display Board

Background—rust, natural hessian or yellow. Border of leaves or leaf shapes. Leaf mobiles. Leaf words on paper leaf shapes, between pictures. Leaf pictures on white paper in variety of techniques and shades of Autumn colour, backed on black or deep Autumn colour for definition. 'Autumn leaves'—orange/yellow lettering on brown.

Display Table

Matching or toning fabric. Books on trees and leaves; collection of sorted leaves and corresponding nuts or fruits.

spiders

Discussion and Observation/Science Ideas

Talk about kinds of spiders, poisonous and non-poisonous; habitat, size, movements. Look for webs and examine pattern of construction. Observe spiders in captivity—in zoo, or vivarium at school.

Art and Craft

Spider paintings—first paint web, or make with glued-on wool or string; stick painted spider on web.

Drawing—from observation—felt pen, pencil, charcoal or conté crayon.

Pictures of spider rhymes—'Little Miss Muffet, 'Incy Wincy Spider'—in paint, or as fabric collage.

Web patterns—black felt tip, crayon, paint (with narrow brush) or construct in wool or string on board stuck with nails, or over felt with contrast thread.

Model spiders in clay, playdough, paper junk.

Maths

Groups and patterns of eight; octagons; tessellations.
Play 'Incy Wincy Spider' counting game (Orchard Toys).

Display Board

Background—dark blue paper. Central web in white/silver wool or string stapled onto board. Large paper spider. Individual pictures round central web. Spider mobiles. 'Spiders'—black lettering on white.

Display Table

Model spiders. Vivarium containing spiders (put in earth, stones, twigs and small insects for food), books, spider game, spider plant.

Other Language Ideas

Words with prefix 'oct'.
Read or tell legend of 'Arachne' for children to re-tell in their own words.

Movement

Spider-like movements: scuttling, scurrying, stopping suddenly and keeping very still. Miming spider rhymes.

Books and Stories

Aranea, Jenny Wagner, Picture Puffin.
The Very Busy Spider, Eric Carle, Hamish Hamilton.
Spiders, Macdonald Starters.
'The Garden Spider', Julia Hutchinson, *Zigzags*, Basil Blackwell.

Poems and Rhymes

'Little Miss Muffet', Traditional.
'Incy Wincy Spider', Traditional.
'The Spider and the Fly', Mary Howitt, *Once Upon a Rhyme*.

bones

Discussion and Observation/Science Ideas

Look at model skeletons—human and other animals'—talk about function, shape, structure and feel. Why are some bones longer/thicker? Discuss fractures, x-rays, different joints. What can be discovered by scientists about a person from bone examinations? (sex, age, health).

Art and Craft

Line drawing from observation—black on white/white on black—crayon, chalk, felt tip, conté crayon.
Skeleton pictures from: spent matchsticks, straws, varieties of pasta, white gummed paper; printing with side of lolly stick or card, and cotton reel for skull. 3D skeletons with pipecleaners or wire.

Maths

Counting ribs, vertebrae, metatarsals. Measuring longest and shortest bones.

Other Language Ideas

Some of the simpler names of bones: spine, skull, ribcage, pelvic girdle, femur etc.

Display Board

Background—black and white chequerboard or bright colour. Individual pictures surrounding full size (luminous) card skeleton. Mount white on black edging, and black on white. 'Bones'—white on black.

Display Table

Paper or fabric to match board. Terraced display of animal skulls, children's toy skeletons, joke skulls, skeleton books and a book of children's writing.

Music-Making

'Skeleton' music, making sounds of clattering bones to various rhythm patterns and ostinati—or to accompany a skeleton story such as 'Funnybones'. Try claves, two-tone woodblocks, guiro, castanets, real animal bones (thoroughly cleaned first!) or sticks and wood pieces of various sizes; rubbing corrugated board or washboard with stick.

Movement/Drama

Skeleton dances to children's own music—jerky, string-puppet-like movements.

Books and Stories

Funnybones, Janet and Allan Ahlberg, Picture Lions, Fontana, William Collins & Co. Ltd.
Teeny Tiny and the Witch Woman, Barbara K. Walker, Picture Puffin.

Songs and Music

'Dem Bones', *Treasury of Negro Spirituals*.
'Danse Macabre', Saint-Säens.
'This Old Man', Traditional.

cold colours/jack frost

1. Cold Colours

Discussion and Observation/Science Ideas

What are 'cold colours'? Look at selection of pictures painted in cold colours and discuss why they look cold.

Art and Craft

Colour mixing—using blue and white, blue and black, then all three, to mix as many different shades as possible. Use in patterns—concentric circles graduating from lightest to darkest; spirals, check pattern, painting around a shape—e.g. a tree—starting with lightest shade for the first layer, and finishing with darkest, or vice versa. Collect fabrics and papers in cold colours for collage. Draw pictures or patterns in crayons or oil pastels using 'cold' colours.

2. Jack Frost

Discussion and Observation

Talk about the appearance of frost, its feel and colour. When is it most seen? Where? Look at patterns on glass and leaves. Look at pictures, or real thing. What happens if you breathe on it, or apply other warmth, and why?

Art and Craft

Individual pictures with 'frost' applied afterwards—white sand, glitter. Large 'Jack Frost' figure drawn by children, with spiky border and spiky clothes—use long paper triangles in white, silver and pale blue, stuck down so that they overlap.

Other Language Ideas

'Frosty' words—nip, freeze, sparkle, crackle.

Poems and Rhymes

'Jack Frost in the Garden', John P. Smeeton, *Come Follow Me*.
'Jack Frost', Gabriel Setoun, *The Book of a Thousand Poems*.

Songs and Music

'Look out, look out!' Carey Bonner, *Child Songs*.
'Ho! Jack Frost', *Harlequin*.
'Little Jacky Jack Frost', *Singing Fun*.

Picture to look at

'Hoarfrost: The Old Road to Ennery Pontoise, 1873', Camille Pissarro

Display Board

1. Cold colours—Background—blue backing paper on board. Mount pictures in black or white. Drape fabric in shades of blue, white and grey from edge of board on to display table underneath. Collect objects in cold colours.

2. Jack Frost—Background of blue or grey printed with silver paint in a spiky fashion. Border of silver foil triangle spikes. Jack Frost in centre; pictures backed in black, white or silver. 'Frost' words. 'Jack Frost'—white (with silver glitter sprinkled on) on blue foil cut in zigzags around edge.

winter clothes

Discussion and Observation/Science Ideas

Discuss seasons: different kinds of winter weather; temperature; ways of keeping warm—food, heating, clothes (importance of layers); insulation. Look at children's outdoor clothes. Discuss suitability of different fabrics for protection against wind, wet and cold.

Art and Craft

Paintings or collage of children in rain/snow/wind in appropriate clothing.

Boot and shoe prints in different colours.

Draw or paint pattern detail from jumper, scarf or hat—or design own pattern, drawing shape of garment first.

Cut out when finished. Weave tiny scarf in wool or string.

Maths

Grouping articles of clothing according to size, fabrics, function, colour.

Pairs: groups of 2 gloves, legwarmers, boots.

Patterns—see under Art and Craft section.

Display Board

Background—grey sky; white for snow below. Silver lametta for rain, stretched taut and stapled onto board diagonally. Cotton wool snow flakes. Children draw round each other to make lifesize figures, then 'clothe' them (paint, fabric or real old clothes) in winter clothes.

Display Table

Grey or white shiny fabric. Display of children's and adults' winter clothes, labelled. Books about clothes.

Play matching games with foot and shoe prints.

Jumble gloves and find the pair.

Other Language Ideas

Vocabulary—sole, waterproof, ribbing, cuff, hood, wrap, collar etc. Names of fabrics.

Movement/Drama

Mime being out in snow, wind and rain—shivering, jumping, stamping feet, blowing hands. Link with—

Music-Making

Find ways of making weather sounds—howling wind, rain, thunder, crunching through snow. Use voices, body percussion, paper—crumpling, tearing, scratching; wire brushes against tins.

Books and Stories

Books about clothes.

Poems and Rhymes

'There's Snow on the Fields', Christina Rossetti, *Come Follow Me*.

Songs and Music

'Clothes', Brenda Piper, *Sing as You Grow*.

birds in winter

Discussion and Observation/Science Ideas

Discuss types of birds to be seen; migration; feeding—reasons why birds need a little help; what to feed and how. Set up a bird table, observe and record birds that feed and which foods are preferred.

Art and Craft

Individual bird pictures—some of which can be cut out and used in display—from observation, or using photographs as guide, or from fantasy. Use fabric collage, feather collections, wood shavings, wool, curled paper, overlapping layers of fringed tissue; also crayon and felt tip pens, or paint using fine brushes. Bird models from junk.

Maths

Counting birds on bird table at set times each day. Number of each kind seen. Largest and smallest birds. Weigh amounts of food given in grammes.

Other Language Ideas

Compose letter to RSPB asking for recipes for bird food and other information.

Bird names. Vocabulary—feather, hop, wing, beak, fly, peck etc.

Movement/Drama

Bird-like movements—quick, light steps; hopping, pecking, flying away.

Music-Making

Imitating bird calls (listen to recordings) using voices and instruments.

Books and Stories

Books about birds.

Poems and Rhymes

'Who?' Florence Hoatson, *Come Follow Me*.
'The Birds on the School Windowsill', Evelyn Dainty, *Come Follow Me*.

Songs and Music

'My Pigeon House', *High Road of Song*.
'The North Wind Shall Blow'. Traditional.

Pictures to look at

R.S.P.B. posters.

Display Board

Pale blue sky, rag-rolled in deeper blue (dip rag in paint and roll or wipe gently but randomly over surface).

Bare trees—torn paper, painted brown.

Snow on ground—white paint, then potato and sponge print in just the faintest tinge of palest blue.

Bird table—Tape together and paint cardboard tubes. Bury one end in wide box weighted with stones or sand. Glue to other end a cutdown and painted cereal box to form bird table. Cover display table and weighted box with white sheeting. Display also bird models, bowls of bird food, greetings cards and tea towels with appropriate motifs; also books, and book of children's writing.

candles

Discussion and Observation/Science Ideas

Talk about occasions for using candles at home and elsewhere; candles in history; how candles are made, and the materials used. Discuss the colour, shape, sizes, scent. Light a candle and talk about what happens—flame, wax, smell.

Art and Craft

Make new candles from collection of old candle stumps.

Decorate plain candles with glitter, sequins, melted wax crayon. Crayon drawings of lighted candle, from observation. Pictures in crayon or paint, of candlelit scenes—birthday, Hallowe'en, Christmas, church, dinner etc.

Draw and decorate candle of own design—use foils, glitter, coloured shapes, felt tip and sequins, with flames in gold foil or glitter.

Maths

Sort by size, shape, colour, e.g. sets—of thin candles, or cake candles.

Time taken to burn down to given heights *or* how far each candle burns in, say, two minutes.

Other Language Activities

Describe favourite candles from those seen. Vocabulary—light, shine, flicker, glow.

Songs and Music

'Light our Candles', *The Trapp Family Recorder Method Book 1.*
'Hanukah', *Harlequin.*
'Diwali', *Tinderbox.*

Display Board

Background—golden yellow or orange paper. Large central candle shape of white paper with 'candle' words on. Surround with individual pictures backed in white or black, and gold 'rays'. Border of gold tinsel.

Display Table

Matching fabric, terraced with boxes. Collection of different candles and own made and decorated candles. Books about lighting and candlemaking.

christmas food

Christmas food

Can you see:
a fork, gravy, pudding,
fish, a cracker,
a ball, sprouts,
or cake?

Our Christmas cake

Discussion and Observation/Science Ideas

Why do we have special food at Christmas? Discuss what the children eat at that time. Compare winter festivals in other cultures, and their food. Talk about origins of traditions—mince pies, turkeys, goose, cake, puddings. List ingredients for cake and pudding. Where and how are they grown?

Art and Craft

Collages made from magazine pictures and advertisements for Christmas food. Paintings of Christmas dinner. Fabric collage meals, matching fabric colour, texture and pattern to the food represented.

Maths

Charts of favourite foods. Weigh cake ingredients. Time the cooking of cake and other foods. Lay the table—1 to 1 correspondence; groups of 4 or 5 knives, forks etc.

Other Language Ideas

Games: 'For my Christmas dinner I ate . . .', in turn each child accumulating more things to remember. Cooking vocabulary—words that rhyme with 'beat', 'chop', 'cake' etc.
Descriptive writing of how cake/mince pies are made.

Cooking

Make cake, mince pies, biscuits, pudding etc. . . . small groups or class activity as appropriate (recipe suggestions on following page).
Make own mini Christmas dinner—each child brings chicken leg, or wing, or even a sausage, to roast: school could provide potatoes and peas.

Poems and Rhymes

'Christmas Pudding', Anon, *Rhyme Time*.
'Mincemeat', Elizabeth Gould, *Come Follow Me*.
'Pudding Charms', Charlotte Druitt, *Come Follow Me*.

Songs and Music

'The Wassail of Figgy Duff', *Merrily to Bethlehem*.
'Gloucestershire Wassail', *Merrily to Bethlehem*.
'We Wish You a Merry Christmas', *Carol Gaily Carol*.

Display Board

Background of red; gold tinsel border. Words 'Christmas food' in white backed in gold foil with zigzag edge. Individual pictures backed in black, white or deep green, surrounding large fabric or paper collage of Christmas cake.

Display Table

Red cloth, shiny fabric if possible—could be cheap acetate lining material. Large 3D dinner—turkey leg shape formed in wire first, covered with layers of newsprint pasted on; or narrow strips of sheeting painted with dilute PVA medium. Paint golden brown when bone dry: 'varnish' using PVA. Potatoes—papier mâché or modelling dough, baked hard, painted and coated with varnish. Sprouts—green tissue and crêpe crumpled firmly—outer 'leaves' glued on outside. Or use hardbaked, painted dough for centres. Large plate from white card; also giant knife and fork (spray silver or cover with kitchen foil). Pudding—pieces of sponge painted brown, dried and stuck together with PVA. Mix custard-coloured paint with PVA and a little water and pour over.

Book describing cake-making. Large decorated cracker. Paper hats and Christmas paper napkins.

Suggested Recipes

Christmas biscuits.
200g./8 oz. self-raising flour
100g./4oz. caster sugar
100g./4 oz. butter or margarine
1 egg, beaten
juice of ½ lemon

- Mix flour and sugar. Rub in fat.
- Add lemon juice and enough egg to make a stiff dough.
- Roll out thinly and cut into shapes.
- Place on greased baking trays and bake for about 15 minutes (Gas Mark 4, 180°C, 350°F).
- When cool, biscuits could be iced and decorated with silver balls, sugar strands etc.

Shortbread
175g./6 oz. plain flour
100g./4 oz. hard margarine
50g./2 oz. sugar

- Place all ingredients in a large mixing bowl. Chop margarine and rub in with fingertips.
- Knead to form a ball.
- Pat out onto greased tray.
- Bake for 20–25 minutes (Gas Mark 4, 180°C, 350°F).

christmas trees

Discussion and Observation

Talk about why we decorate fir trees at Christmas. Look at them growing—touch and smell. Look at pictures of decorated Christmas trees for ideas; also shop decorations.

Decoration Ideas/Display Table

'Solid shapes' tree—collect old boxes, packets and balls, and decorate lavishly with paint and PVA, foils, sequins, sweet wrappers, glitter, bottle tops, mosaics of small squares of bright wrapping paper, pasta stuck on boxes and sprayed silver and gold, ribbons. Use loops of Sellotape, sticky fixers or staple guns to attach to tree.

Bright background—red or yellow with matching cover for display table. 'Solid shapes presents' under tree.

Word Tree—cut out appropriate shape for word.

and decorate with the word written in bright crayon.

Other words—bauble, ball, heart, bird, tub, ribbon, tinsel.

Children tree: each child draws small picture of her or himself, and clothes it in bright crayon, fabric or paper scraps, with name across middle (as illustrated on following page).

Colour tree—decorate in shades of one colour—either homemade or bought decorations (or both).

The tree itself: Any—artificial green one or real one on the table, or two dimensional tree with layers of fringed green crêpe and tissue for needles: the whole tree curved outwards from wall to give 3D effect; or print paper in different greens with edge of card.

Individual tree pictures: Fabric or paper collage, or use desiccated coconut or rice dyed green with food colouring.

Books and Stories

'The Little Match Girl', Hans Andersen
'The Fir Tree', Hans Andersen

Poems and Rhymes

'Little Tree', E. E. Cummings, *Rhyme Time.*
'Advice to a Child'. Eleanor Farjeon, *Rhyme Time.*
'Ten Little Christmas Trees', Rodney Bennett, *The Book of a Thousand Poems.*

Songs and Music

'O Christmas Tree', *Carol Gaily Carol.*
'See the Little Christmas Tree', *High Road of Song.*
'Deep in the Woods', *Nursery Songbook,* W. E. Barnard.

Pictures to look at

Any magazine pictures or shop displays of decorated Christmas trees.

Who are the fairies
on our Christmas tree?

cinderella

Discussion and Observation

Read a good version (e.g. Charles Perrault) with attractive illustrations. Listen to a story tape. See it as a play or pantomime. Talk about characters. Why were sisters so bad-tempered and unkind? What is a stepmother? Why wasn't Cinderella unpleasant to her stepsisters in return?

Art and Craft

Individual paintings, collage and mosaics using plenty of bright and exotic papers and fabrics for ball dresses—sequins, glitter, sweet wrappers, foils, tinsel.

Maths

Shoe sizes: Make or borrow tiny shoe or ballet shoe and spray or paint silver or cover with glitter. Put on velvet cushion. Borrow foot-measuring gauge for children to compare shoe sizes or put paper cut-outs of each child's feet on chart or wall. Group feet into those who would fit Cinderella's slipper and those who would not, after sending group of children around classes with the shoe.

Other Language Ideas

Re-telling story verbally or in written form in own way. Vocabulary of story. Family relationships.

Music-Making/Movement/Drama

Mime story using different instruments for each character and appropriate sound effects for each event in story.

Books and Stories

Compare a few different versions. Which do the children like best, and why?

Poems and Rhymes

'Coach', Eleanor Farjeon, *Puffin Quartet of Poets*.

Display Board

Background—yellow paper stippled with deeper yellow for subtle textured effect. Floor—bright red, with pattern of leaf-prints in darker red. Children draw, paint and clothe characters—sisters' dresses can be gaudy and bright—Cinderella's sooty and drab. Drape real fabric on the right for curtain hiding Fairy Godmother.

Display Table

Cover left half with red fabric, right half with grey cloth or torn and dirty hessian. Modern cleaning equipment (unavailable to Cinderella) on left. Label where appropriate. Cinderella books.

christmas plants

Discussion and Observation/Science Ideas

Look at bunches of holly, ivy and mistletoe. Talk about legends and stories behind each plant, and the reason for their association with Christmas. Discuss texture, shape, colour, berries and habitat.

Art and Craft

Pictures in gummed paper. Drawings in crayon or felt tip. Paper collage, using different Christmas wrapping papers.
Painting from observation, mixing various shades of green and using fine brushes.
Paintings of background legends.

Maths

Shape pictures—diamonds for holly; triangles for ivy; ovals for mistletoe; circles for berries.
Make patterns using these shapes.

Other Language Ideas

Find five ways to describe each plant.
Choose missing words, e.g. 'Holly feels soft/prickly'; 'Mistletoe has white/red berries.'

Books and Stories

Stories of our Christmas Customs, N. F. Pearson, Ladybird.
'The holly bears a berry', *Stories for Christmas*, Alison Uttley, Puffin.

Poems and Rhymes

'The Computer's First Christmas Card', *A Single Star* compiled by David Davis.
'Holly Red and Mistletoe White', Alison Uttley, *A Single Star*.
'Welcome Yule', George Wither, *A Single Star*.

Songs and Music

'The Holly and the Ivy', Traditional.
'Deck the Hall', Welsh Christmas Song, *The Easiest Book of Christmas Carols*, E. F. Pike.

Display Board

Sponge print or daub 'snow' in white paint over background of red or blue. Large picture of holly, ivy or mistletoe, with leaves cut out by children in gummed or other suitable heavy paper. Papier mâché berries painted and coated with PVA. Branches/twigs of thin wire bound with crêpe, stapled to board. *Or* individual pictures of the plants on white paper—backed in red or green on contrasting background. Border of printed holly shapes round edge of board (diamonds and circles).

advent calendar

Discussion and Observation

Bring one or two bought Advent calendars to look at and compare with other through-the-year calendars.

Maths

Ordinal and cardinal numbers.
Months in year: number of days in month.
Snakes and Ladders game.
Number square.

Display Board

Giant Advent calendar—may be divided into any number of appropriate squares—days till end of term, school concert, party, Christmas Day etc. Children make each picture individually or in pairs, plus a decorated cover with a number on it. Pictures could be based on themes such as toys, portraits of children in the class, food, clothing, animals or Christmas motifs—bell, tree, candle, Father Christmas, reindeer, pudding etc. The pictures should be bright, clear and simple, in paint, felt tip, bright paper or foils, glitter or crayon thickly applied. Pictures are then stapled to wall with borders of crêpe or foil, and covers stapled on top and removed altogether each day. Alternatively, covers could form a winter or Christmas snow scene with doors cut in them over each picture. It can be very effective to have a specific colour scheme, e.g. red, white and green, as illustrated.

Other Language Ideas

Class diary of events in large book, until last day of term.

Songs and Music

'The Twelve Days of Christmas', *Number Rhymes*.
'The Calendar to Advent', *Sing as you Grow*, Brenda Piper.

shiny things

Discussion and Observation/Science Ideas

Talk about surfaces and textures—dull, shiny, smooth, rough. Look for shiny things everywhere: e.g. decorations, jewellery, coins, foil, cutlery, tools, patent leather, glass, mirrors, clothes, woods etc. Collect things that create shine (empty or well-sealed containers only, or use labels)—nail varnish, PVA, gloss paint, varnish, wax polish, window cleaner, metal polish, book cover film. Collect rusty objects: discuss the causes of rust, and ways of treating it.

Art and Craft

Individual pictures using different techniques. Collages of—coloured foils and sweet wrappers, sequins, bottle tops, polythene pieces (from different coloured carrier bags).

Foil relief: On piece of card, stick buttons, jar lids, string, sandpaper, anything with interesting shape or textured pattern. Spread with PVA and then cover with foil so it takes the shape of the relief. For extra contrast of dark and shine, rub a layer of black shoe polish into picture and gently wipe off the top—black will stay in the 'hollows'.

Display Board

Background—plain bright yellow and blue in a chequerboard pattern. Border of silver or gold foil round edge. Mount individual pictures on black or white for contrast. Hang mirror in centre (or star as shown) and position pictures around it. Label mirror 'Can you see your reflection?' 'Shiny things'—silver lettering on white.

Display Table

Cover with shiny fabric if possible (e.g. cheap acetate lining) in yellow or orange. Group things appropriately and label with folded cards.

Maths

Group collection into sets according to use or composition—or shape.

Other Language Ideas

Vocabulary—reflection, bright, shining, gleaming, smooth, cool.
Other pairs of opposites—heavy, light; big, small; cold, hot, etc.

Cookery

Have a shiny food party—make jelly, toffee apples, roast or fried food.

Books and Stories

'King Midas and the Golden Touch' Traditional.
'The Silver Shilling', Hans Andersen
'Rumplestiltskin', Traditional.

Poems and Rhymes

'Shining Things', Elizabeth Gould, *Come Follow Me*.

Songs and Music

'The Mirror', *Singing Games II*, Herbert Wiseman and Sydney Northcote.
'The Shiny Little House', *Third Sixty Songs for Little Children*.

bells

Discussion and Observation/Science Ideas

What is a bell? Where are they found and heard? Discuss different kinds, size, uses (signal, warning, celebration, mourning). Collect as many bells as possible. Look at and listen to church or school bells and Big Ben. Compare sounds.

Art and Craft

Bell mobiles and decorations—yoghurt pots and similar, covered in foil, newsprint, paint and PVA; then tinsel, sequins and glitter. Hang bead inside.

Collage of bell shapes, using different papers.

Drawings of bells in felt tip, crayon, charcoal, chalk.

Paintings of situations in which bells are heard—weddings, on board ship, Big Ben, school, old fire engines, doorbells.

Print bell shapes with thick card, or bell shape cut into a large potato.

Richly decorate paper bell shapes—mosaic of foil or gummed paper squares, glitter, sequins, crayons.

Maths

Group bells according to weight, colour or height; or according to sound in ascending or descending order. Measure circumference and height.

Other Language Ideas

'Bell' words—ring, chime, knell, peal, ding dong, clang, tinkle.
Words that rhyme with 'bell'.

Music-Making

Find other instruments that have bell-like sounds—chime bars, triangle, glockenspiel. Improvise simple tunes using bell collection.

Books and Stories

Dick Whittington, Traditional.

Poems and Rhymes

'The Bells of London', Anon, *Come Follow Me*.
'The Bells', Edgar Allan Poe, *Puffin Book of Verse*.
'Silver Bells', Hamish Hendry, *The Book of a Thousand Poems*.
'Oranges and Lemons', Traditional.

Songs and Music

'10 Little Jingle Bells', *Singing Fun*.
'Jingle Bells', Traditional.
'Wand of Youth', Elgar (Suite No. 2—*Little Bells*).

Display Board

Bright background—yellow, red or white. Border of gold tinsel and gold foil paper, or green with red shiny berries as illustrated. Bell pictures mounted in black or red. Bell poem. Bell mobiles hung from ceiling. 'Bells'—in red foil lettering on green.

Display Table

Matching fabric. Bell collection, labelled where appropriate.

snow

Discussion and Observation/Science Ideas

Talk about what snow is; where it comes from; its feel, its appearance when falling and when it has settled; cold countries; games to play in the snow; snow crystals; melting snow. Examine the snow with a magnifying glass.

Art and Craft

Snowflake shapes (six pointed) cut from doilies, and circles of blue, white and silver paper in various sizes. Decorate with glitter or sequins and use in collages. Stick one on each side of paper circles, cut to the same circumference as the snowflakes, and hang as mobiles.

Snow scenes from observation—white chalk, paint, or crayon on black paper.

Pictures in fabric or paper collage using pieces of torn paper, polystyrene pieces, cottonwool, flaked rice or white wool as snow, or printed with fingertips, ends of dowel or lightly flicked from brush.

Individual 3D snowmen using painted papier mâché body and cottonwool, or smaller papier mâché head, or form basic wire frame in shape of snowman, wind strips of old sheeting firmly round, painting each layer with thin coat of plaster of Paris, allowing to dry between coats. Glue on or paint features when finished.

Simpler 3D snowmen: Upturned yoghurt pots covered in rumpled white tissue or cotton wool or covered with glued desiccated coconut. Glue on polystyrene or pingpong ball for head and add features.

Maths

Melting—put saucers of snow in different places of varying temperatures. Note time taken to thaw—which was quickest and why?

Weigh snow, comparing weight to volume—e.g. 'x grammes of snow made x mls. water', *or* 'filled x small cups'.

Patterns and groups of 6 (on squared paper).

Hexagons.

Other Language Ideas

'Snow vocabulary—blizzard, drift, flake, flurry, thaw, sleet, slush etc.

Children's own snow stories: descriptions of snow; what they like playing in the snow. Own magic snowmen stories.

Movement/Drama

Mime—building snowman—rolling snow into large ball, patting and shaping. Throwing snowballs, walking in snow.

Books and Stories

The Snowman, © Raymond Briggs, 1978, Hamish Hamilton.
The Snowman, Hans Andersen.
Snow. Macdonald Starters.
The Snow Queen, Hans Andersen, Picture Puffin.

Poems and Rhymes

'Snow', Walter de la Mare, *Once Upon a Rhyme*.
'Who', Lillian Moore, *Once Upon a Rhyme*.
'Death of a Snowman', Vernon Scannell, *First Poetry Book*.

Songs and Music

'Snowflakes', *Harlequin*.
'Sledging', *Harlequin*.
'Snow' from 'The Seasons, Complete Ballet', by Glazunov,
Philharmonia Orchestra.

Pictures to look at

'Snowstorm', J. M. W. Turner, 1842 (National Gallery.)
'Sunshine and Snow, Lavacourt, 1881', Monet.
'Snow at Louveciennes, 1874', Pissarro

Display Board

Either snow scene—textured white paint sprinkled with glitter; children draw or paint and clothe themselves in warm clothes—fabric or paper scraps, and arrange on background. Snow-covered houses and trees. 'Snow'-white lettering on blue.
or enormous snowman, textured and glittered on blue background. Could surround it with individual pictures.

Display Table

Cover with blue or white fabric; books, clothes with snow or snowman motifs, model snowmen.

robins

Discussion and Observation/Science Ideas

Talk about appearance, size, feeding and nesting habits, egg colour, friendliness, song. Visit museum or look at pictures of robins. Why is it regarded as a Christmas bird? Collect cards and wrapping paper with robin motifs.

Art and Craft

Draw in crayon, felt tipped pen or pastel.

Using texture—thick combed paint, or small strips of tissue or fringed tissue, stuck in overlapping layers.

Collages in pulses and grains stuck with PVA. Leave in natural colours or paint when dry.

Line drawings in charcoal, felt tip, pencil, crayon or white paper.

Bird pictures on white paper or previously painted backgrounds of sky and grass.

Display Board

Background—bright yellow, red, emerald green or white paper. Row of 'shape' robins at top. Individual robin pictures backed in black or white or red. Word 'Robins'—red lettering on brown.

Display Table

Matching cover; junk robin models; Christmas cards; boxes, wrapping paper etc. with robin designs or motifs; bird books.

Maths

Make 'shape' birds (circles and triangles)

Other Language Ideas

Factual writing about the robin, to go in a book.

Poems and Rhymes

'Gay Robin is seen no more', Robert Bridges, *Come Follow Me*.
'Robin's Song', Rodney Bennett, *Come Follow Me*.
'Who Killed Cock Robin?' Traditional.

Songs and Music

'When the Red Red Robin', *Ta-ra-ra boom-de-ay*.
'Robin in the Rain', *High Road of Song*.
'The North Wind Shall Blow', Traditional.

index

notes

notes

notes

For sales and distribution outside America:
  Folens Publishers, Albert House, Apex Business Centre,
  Boscombe Road, Dunstable, Beds., LU5 4RL, England

BELAIR PUBLICATIONS USA
116 Corporation Way
Venice, Florida 34292

For details of other Belair Publications
please write to:
Belair Publications Ltd.
P.O. Box 12
Twickenham TW1 2QL, England

notes